ANIMALS THAT CHANGED THE WORLD

BY KELTIE THOMAS

annick press
toronto + new york + vancouver

© 2010 Keltie Thomas (text)
Map on pages 4–5 by Tina Holdcroft

Designed by Sheryl Shapiro

Annick Press Ltd.

All rights reserved. No part of this work covered by the copyrights hereon may be reproduced or used in any form or by any means — graphic, electronic, or mechanical — without the prior written permission of the publisher.

We acknowledge the support of the Canada Council for the Arts, the Ontario Arts Council, and the Government of Canada through the Canada Book Fund (CBF) for our publishing activities.

 ONTARIO ARTS COUNCIL
CONSEIL DES ARTS DE L'ONTARIO

Cataloging in Publication

Thomas, Keltie
        Animals that changed the world / by Keltie Thomas.

Includes bibliographical references and index.
ISBN 978-1-55451-243-0 (bound).—ISBN 978-1-55451-242-3 (pbk.)

        1. Animals—Juvenile literature. I. Title.

QL49.T55 2010   j590   C2010-903119-9

Distributed in Canada by:
Firefly Books Ltd.
66 Leek Crescent
Richmond Hill, ON
L4B 1H1

Published in the U.S.A. by Annick Press (U.S.) Ltd.
Distributed in the U.S.A. by:
Firefly Books (U.S.) Inc.
P.O. Box 1338
Ellicott Station
Buffalo, NY 14205

Printed in China.

Visit us at: www.annickpress.com

for readers who will
change the world
—K.T.

Contents

What makes our world different than any other known in the universe?

Birds fly in the sky, fish swim in the sea, and lots of other animals walk, run, and crawl over the land. Our world is animals' only known romping and stomping ground. What's more, as animals romp, stomp, and tromp, eat, poop, and fart—and work for people—they are changing the world as we know it.

Sound far-fetched? Animals have changed the world since they first set foot, paw, and claw on Earth. Long ago, the ancient ancestors of animals and all living things, microbes called bacteria, created an atmosphere on Earth that allowed life to thrive and evolve into the animals, plants, and people you know today.

That's not all. Animals have led our ancient ancestors to explore the world, trampled and chowed down whole fields, creating deserts in their wake, killed millions of people as "secret agents" of disease, and even separated the rich from the poor.

Get set to discover all this and more in this book of animals that changed the world.

4

EUROPE

ASIA

PACIFIC
OCEAN

AFRICA

INDIAN
OCEAN

AUSTRALIA

CHAPTER 1

DINER

Partners in Time

You know your local burger joint? Chances are it wouldn't exist if there were no cows. Nor would the thick, juicy burgers and frothy milkshakes it serves up from the meat and milk of cows. Nor would any of the umpteen other burger joints that crowd streets around the world and continue to pop up everywhere.

All the world's beefy burgers and creamy milkshakes come from a partnership our Stone Age ancestors forged with cattle by taming and herding those animals thousands of years ago. What's more, the ancients may never have taken in cattle like this if they hadn't had some success herding goats and sheep first. That's because aurochs, the wild cattle that roamed Earth back in the Stone Age, were dangerous characters—er, creatures—to run into at the local watering hole, or anywhere else for that matter.

Turn the page to go back in time and get the goods on goats, sheep, and cattle. Discover how these animals became people's partners, walking through the world with our Stone Age ancestors and changing the face of continents along the way.

THE GOAT

Meet the goat—a.k.a. the "poor man's cow." The two-horned creature earned this nickname because it doesn't need a rich environment to live. The goat can thrive in harsh places where few other animals can survive. Not only did this hardiness allow ancient goats to go wherever our Stone Age ancestors went, it also helped our ancestors survive along the way. Check out how goats and people have changed the world as partners through time.

MUG SHOT

Names: "Billy goat" or "buck" for males, "doe" or "nanny" for females, and "kid" for young goats
Domestication Date: Stone Age, about 10,000 years ago
Number in the World Today: 790 million
In the Wild: Ibex and markhor
Claim to Fame: A goat can provide everything you need to survive—meat, milk, clothing, fat to burn for light, bones and sinew for building things, and poop for fuel.

The Goat

Goat skin

Ibex goat

Did you know that more people around the world drink goat milk than cow milk?

A Walking Lunchbox

Nobody knows why exactly or even how, but about 10,000 years ago goats began living in the company of people. Not only did our Stone Age ancestors tame the wild creatures, but they also began keeping and breeding herds of goats. Back then, people lived off the land, hunting and gathering food. They moved from place to place in search of meals as herds of buffalo and other animals migrated with the change of seasons. There were no fridges or even tin cans in which people could store meat to keep it from rotting. So they were constantly on the lookout for a fresh supply. But once people began keeping goats, they had a "walking lunchbox" that could trot along with them wherever they went. What's more, people began using goatskins to store food and carry water on the road. And this changed the world by allowing people to travel farther without having to stop to hunt for dinner, and also to hunt less often because they had a fresh supply of meat on hand. Is it any wonder goats and other farm animals are known as "livestock"?

FACT TRACK

Ancient rock paintings in the Sahara Desert show elephants, giraffes, and cattle grazing on grassy plains. Archaeologists think this shows that the Sahara was once lush with grass and had much more rain than it does today.

HOME IS WHERE THE FOOD IS

As people began to raise goats, they no longer needed to follow herds of migrating animals to hunt for meat. They began to settle down and live in one place. Villages sprung up where people made homes and herded goats. That's not all. The goats helped people farm and grow crops. No kidding! Ancient Egyptian farmers not only kept herds of goats but let them loose in the fields at planting time to trample seeds into the ground. As the amount of goats, a.k.a. livestock, and crops grew, people were able to feed more people. Villages grew into towns, and towns grew into cities. Eventually, not everyone had to raise livestock or grow their own food. Some people were free to do other jobs. Over time, they invented new tools, technology, and even writing. Others were free to make art and make war. What's more, since people were no longer on the move all the time, they no longer had to carry all their belongings. So they were free to make bigger things. Over time, they made tables and chairs, bathtubs, grand pianos, spinning wheels, looms, the printing press, and even the world's first computer—which was the size of an entire room. People also began to collect more stuff.

Ancient Egyptians kept goats as livestock. One pharaoah even had 2,134 goats buried with him.

Raising livestock gave people more time on their hands. Then they could make and play things like the piano and invent machines like the printing press.

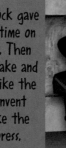

Deserts: A Goat's Breakfast?

Despite what you may have heard, goats do not eat tin cans, red shirts, or even garbage. Goats are picky eaters. The four-legged critters refuse to eat food that's been soiled, trampled, or even on the ground. They prefer leaves and twigs to grass. In fact, when goats chow down, they start munching from the top down. They nibble seed heads or leaves at the top of shrubs and trees and eat their way to the bottom. In the process, they can kill the plants.

Today, some scientists think that as our ancient ancestors kept herds of goats close to home in places like the Sahara and the Middle East, the goats gobbled up all the plants, expanding existing deserts. Ancient farmers may even have used the gobbling power of goats to clear land for crops. With no plants, there were no roots to hold topsoil in place or keep it moist. The topsoil dried out and blew away. Without topsoil, plants couldn't grow and land turned to desert. Deserts like the Sahara grew in size and, over time, the huge desert began to influence the world's climate. Today, for example, many hurricanes that hit North America and the eastern Pacific Ocean begin to form over the Sahara Desert. And so goats have left a mark on the world that continues to affect the world today.

HE'S A SCAPEGOAT.

SPEAK OF THE BEAST THIS MEANS HE HAS BEEN BLAMED FOR THE MISTAKES, FAULTS, OR WRONGDOINGS OF OTHERS. THE WORD SCAPEGOAT COMES FROM THE ANCIENT CUSTOM OF SLAUGHTERING GOATS AS A SACRIFICE, OR GIFT, TO THE GODS.

Can you spot the goats in this tree? Believe it or not, goats often climb argan trees in Morocco.

11

SHEEP

Just like goats, sheep were a meal people could take on the road without having to carry it because sheep could follow along on their own four legs. In fact, archaeologists think sheep and goats were domesticated at about the same time. Check out how flocks of woolly sheep formed a close-knit bond with people all over the world.

Bighorn sheep

MUG SHOT

Names: "Ram" for males, "ewe" for females, and "lamb" for young ones
Domestication Date: Stone Age, about 10,000 years ago
Number in the World Today: About 1,060 million
In the Wild: Argali, bighorn, and urial
Claim to Fame: Sheep are gregarious, or sociable. They flock together, like to hang out with a group, and follow a single leader.

Lambs

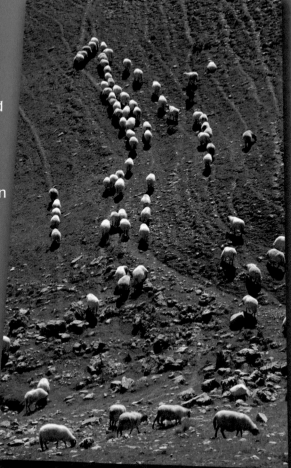

A Penny for Your Flock

Imagine two Stone Age families the exact same size living in a cave side by side. If one had sheep and the other didn't, which do you think would be richer? The one with sheep? No doubt! That's because this family would have more to eat than just the pickings of the latest hunt. What's more, if they had more meat than they needed, they could trade sheep for other things that they needed.

And that's just what people did. The number of sheep or other livestock that people had became a measure of their wealth, and eventually people began to use sheep just like we use money today. Of course, there's no way anyone could carry around a pocketful of sheep—that's one reason coins were invented. Some experts think the world's first silver coin was worth one sheep and others think it was worth 11 of the woolly critters. Whatever the case may be, herding sheep and other livestock made it possible for people to stock up, or accumulate, wealth. Some people became rich. Others became poor. And wealth became something that people, rich or poor, were willing to work, beg, borrow, or even steal for.

Sheep Clothe the World

Once sheep started being kept, bred, and fed by people, a.k.a. domesticated, the animals themselves began to change. No kidding! Their brains shrank, their legs got shorter, and their horns all but disappeared. What's more, their hairy coats turned white and woolly, and white sheep with black or brown faces and legs started to appear. As animals become domesticated, they develop physical characteristics different from their wild ancestors. In fact, differences like these that show up in animal bones help archaeologists tell when particular animals became domesticated. Soon, people began to collect wool as sheep shed it, and even to shear wool right off sheep. They learned how to spin sheep's wool into yarn, make the yarn into warm clothes, and sell wool clothes to make a living. And so a "golden fleece" from the backs of sheep spun into the world and began to clothe people everywhere.

SPEAK OF THE BEAST

COUNTING SHEEP

THIS WAY OF HELPING PEOPLE FALL ASLEEP WAS USED AS FAR BACK AS 1854. IT MAY COME FROM SHEPHERDS COUNTING THEIR FLOCK AT NIGHT TO MAKE SURE THEY HAD THE SAME NUMBER OF SHEEP AS THEY DID IN THE MORNING.

Sheep Start a Revolution

By the 1700s, huge flocks of sheep grazed the grasslands of Britain's countryside, where people raised them for wool. Without a bleat, these sheep helped kick off the Industrial Revolution, which swept around the world, as people began making massive amounts of goods with machines in factories. The sheep did their bit by producing large amounts of wool that could be spun into thread for fabric. Spinning thread and weaving it into fabric by hand was a big job that provided work for many people in the countryside. But once spinning machines and automated looms rolled onto the scene, people could use them to turn sheep's wool into fabric faster and in greater quantities than ever before. Soon they could feed the fabric into sewing machines to churn out sweaters, hats, scarves, and other wool goods faster than before. The result? Many people moved from the countryside, where they had made goods by hand, to cities to work in factories, making goods with machines. Machine-made woolen goods flooded markets around the world, factories began turning out many other kinds of goods too, and more people moved to cities to work in the factories, changing the very "fabric" of society.

CATTLE

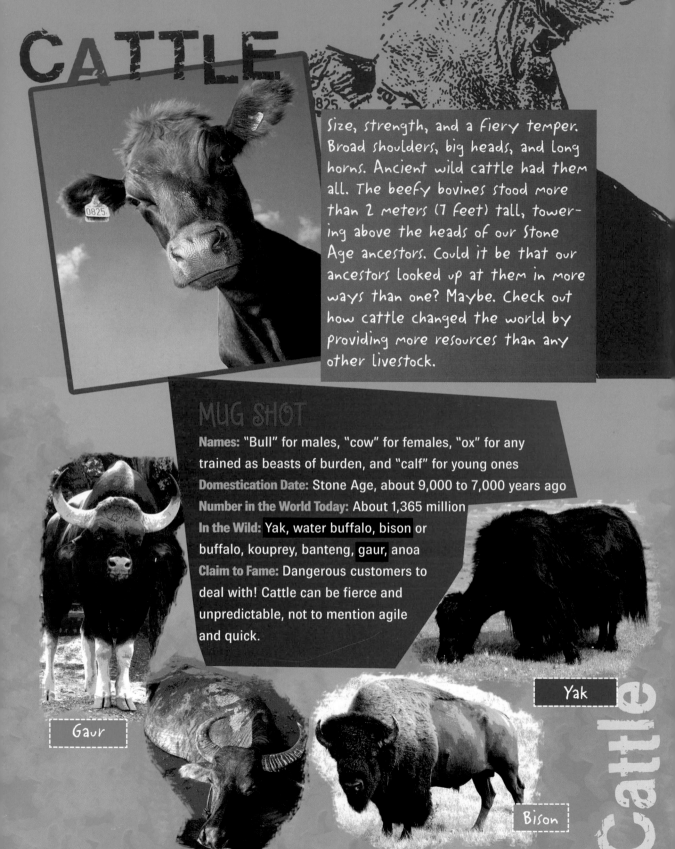

Size, strength, and a fiery temper. Broad shoulders, big heads, and long horns. Ancient wild cattle had them all. The beefy bovines stood more than 2 meters (7 feet) tall, towering above the heads of our Stone Age ancestors. Could it be that our ancestors looked up at them in more ways than one? Maybe. Check out how cattle changed the world by providing more resources than any other livestock.

MUG SHOT

Names: "Bull" for males, "cow" for females, "ox" for any trained as beasts of burden, and "calf" for young ones
Domestication Date: Stone Age, about 9,000 to 7,000 years ago
Number in the World Today: About 1,365 million
In the Wild: Yak, water buffalo, bison or buffalo, kouprey, banteng, gaur, anoa
Claim to Fame: Dangerous customers to deal with! Cattle can be fierce and unpredictable, not to mention agile and quick.

Gaur

Yak

Bison

Water buffalo

The World Screams for Ice Cream

Just who convinced the first cow to let down her milk and how, no one knows. But evidence shows that ancient Egyptians and Mesopotamians were milking cows around 4000 BCE. Sure, goats and sheep can be milked too. But it wasn't until cows' milk began to flow that milk really made a splash around the world. People soon began using cows' milk to make cheese, butter, cream, and eventually whipped cream, creme donuts, crème brûlée, milkshakes, and ice cream to scream for too. Milk contains protein and many other nutrients the human body needs to grow. So drinking milk and eating foods made with milk gave people an advantage because they were able to get the nourishment they needed during times when other nutrient-rich foods became scarce. In fact, drinking milk has even changed human evolution, as many people developed the ability to digest milk as adults. Could it be that we're trying to milk milk for all it's worth?

THE LURE OF MANURE

Plop, plop! Poop, poop! Oh, what a relief it is—for cows and the earth, that is! Cattle manure may create a big stink, but it's an excellent fertilizer for farmers' fields. What's more, it costs nothing for farmers who have cattle and it comes in endless supply. One cow can expel enough dung to fill an entire suitcase in just one day. All farmers have to do is let a herd loose to let loose and dung will drop. Bombs away, as they say! Long ago, cattle poop changed the world by nourishing soil, revitalizing crop fields, and allowing people to grow more food. Burning cowpats also gave Stone Age humans a source of fuel. In fact, people in many parts of the world still burn dung for fuel today, and some power plants make electricity from cattle poop to power up people's homes and gadgets.

Get a load of cow dung.

Wow! Can That Cow Plow!

Meat, milk, and lots of muscle. That's what cattle are made of and how. Around 3000 BCE, oxen were pulling heavy loads and doing farm work in Mesopotamia, modern-day Iraq. Some people think that the brute strength of oxen led to the invention of the plow, a machine farmers use to turn and break up soil for planting. The first ox-drawn plow was likely a simple digging stick that created a rut in the soil as oxen walked through a field dragging it behind them. The plow dug deeper than farmers had been able to before, and the results were extraordinary. Plants put down stronger roots and farmers grew more food than ever before. In fact, farmers grew so much food that they had way more than they needed. So, just like when goats were domesticated, some people no longer had to grow their own food and were free to do other jobs. Eventually, wheels were added to plows. Then oxen could pull plows through heavier soils, such as those in northwestern Europe. And so oxen helped spread farming around the world. In fact, oxen plowed fields and hauled logs for the early settlers of North America as well. They also pulled big covered wagons through mud and rough roads across the continent to open up the Wild West for settlers. And in many parts of the world, oxen still plow farmers' fields today.

SPEAK OF THE BEAST

THAT WON'T HAPPEN TILL THE COWS COME HOME.

IN HUMAN TERMS, THIS MEANS IT WON'T HAPPEN FOR A LONG TIME, IF EVER. THIS SAYING REFERS TO THE SLOW, DILLY-DALLYING WAY COWS MOVE FROM THE FIELD TO THE MILKING ROOM.

Bovine Burps Turn Up the Heat

Did you know that a cow drinks enough water to fill an entire bathtub, snarfs down heaps of food that weigh as much as the average five-year-old kid, and belches almost nonstop every day? No? Well, here's the kicker. When cattle belch, they release a gas called methane, which causes global warming. As methane piles up in Earth's atmosphere—a layer of gases that traps heat from the sun like a blanket—the atmosphere traps more heat and then temperatures rise on the planet.

The average cow burps up about 600 liters (136 gallons) of methane a day. That much methane could fill up 50,000 big round party balloons. And with more than a billion cows on the planet, it really adds up. Scientists estimate that almost one-fifth of all the world's methane emissions comes from cattle and other livestock. Ever since Stone Age cowboys began to raise cattle, the demand for meat has shot up. Today, the average amount of meat eaten in the world is roughly equal to that of one burger per person per day. To meet this demand, we raise more cattle than ever before.

Not only do cattle and other livestock add to global warming, but they also take up nearly one-third of all the world's land for grazing and growing livestock feed. The situation isn't "udderly" hopeless, though. We can all cut down livestock emissions and land use by simply eating less meat.

Make that a fruit burger and veggie burger to go.

FACT TRACK

The daily dung of one cow can supply enough energy to burn a 100-watt lightbulb for one day and then some.

19

ANIMALS DID WHAT?!

What's gotten into my goats? wondered Ethiopian goatherd Kaldi about 1,200 years ago—or so the legend goes. Kaldi's goats were bouncing off the walls—er, bushes—as they jumped from plant to plant, gobbling up red berries. The goats were so unusually lively that Kaldi decided to try the berries himself—and found they gave him extraordinary energy.

Kaldi told an Imam, or holy man, about the invigorating effect of the berries. The Imam thought the berries were evil and flung them into a fire. But then a pleasant aroma began to waft up from the flames. So the Imam rescued the roasted berries, cooled them in water, and drank the brew. The drink was delicious and soon spread around the world.

Sound far-fetched? Well, if this story really gets your goat, you're not alone, for no one knows whether it is fact or fiction. Nevertheless, coffee beans are seeds of a berry, historians say coffee comes from Ethiopia, and today people drink more coffee than any other drink in the world.

Coffee berries

Goats Discovered Coffee

Africa

20

CHAPTER 2

Pets Are the Best

Do you have a pet? Chances are, your answer to this question is "You bet!" In North America, more than half of Canadians and nearly two-thirds of Americans have a pet. Dogs and cats are the most popular ones on the continent and around the world, and hamsters, fish, and guinea pigs are well liked too.

Every day, millions of people pet them, pat them, play with them, cuddle them, coddle them, name them, call them, walk them, talk to them, feed them, chase them, adopt them, train them, skateboard with them, cycle with them, and even fall asleep with them.

The world just wouldn't be the same without them. Find out how some of these fun-loving critters have evolved from wolves, wild cats, and cavies, fought like cats and dogs to change the history of the world—and cracked the case of killer diseases.

THE DOG

Woof! Woof! Heel! Bow-wow! Sit! Do people train dogs or do dogs train people? Maybe it depends whether you're looking at the world through human eyes or canine eyes. Here's how wolves evolved into dogs and forged a bond with people like no other animal.

African wild dogs

Australian dingo

MUG SHOT

Names: "Canine," "mutt" for dogs of no discernible breed, "puppy" for young dogs
Domestication Date: Stone Age, around 15,000 years ago
Number in the World Today: More than 172 million
In the Wild: African wild dogs, dingoes
Claim to Fame: First animal domesticated, or tamed, by humans

LOOK WHO'S COMING TO DINNER?

How did wolves, whose bite is bigger than their bark, come to live in the company of people? The only way to know would be to travel back in time and ask our Stone Age ancestors. Of course, that's impossible. Instead, scientists and archaeologists study ancient remains of our ancestors and their wolfy companions, critter DNA that's like genetic fingerprints, and the world around us to develop theories. One theory is that wolves and people hunted down the same wild game for food. Thus, they often ventured onto each other's turf. Some wolves may have crept close to the people's campfires while meat was roasting to scrounge for scraps and refuse. Eventually, some humans may have adopted wolf pups and, in time, the pups' descendants lost some of their wolf characteristics and evolved into dogs. What's more, the idea that animals could be tamed, or domesticated, was born. And this idea changed the world completely—paving the way, as we've already seen, for goats, sheep, cattle, and other animals to be domesticated, which led to takeout lunches, live-stock, farming, cities, deserts, money, burger joints, milkshakes (see page 7) … and who knows what next.

Italian greyhound

Dogs Join the Hunt

Near the end of the last Ice Age, our ancestors lived by hunting and gathering food. They killed wild game with direct blows from heavy stone axes. But around the same time that they started to have pet dogs yapping at their heels, they began hunting with arrows that they could shoot from a distance. Archaeologists think that dogs may have joined the hunt then to chase down any wounded prey. This would have made the new hunting technique more efficient. Whatever the case may be, dogs proved to be excellent hunters, and people began to breed them for hunting. Evidence shows that ancient Egyptians had hunting dogs that looked like modern greyhounds. People also began using dogs to guard their homes and livestock, herd their animals, and haul heavy loads.

English springer spaniel

A sheepdog keeps sheep in line.

FACT TRACK

Domestic dogs have a much greater ability to bark than wild canines. Scientists think dogs may have evolved this trait to "talk" to people.

24

Fido Likes Me

SPEAK OF THE BEAST

THIS HOUSE IS GOING TO THE DOGS!

THIS HOUSE IS A WRECK! IN THE 1600S, THIS SAYING SPRANG UP TO DESCRIBE SOMETHING SLIDING INTO RUIN. BACK THEN, DOGS DIDN'T HAVE THE CUSHY LIFE MANY ENJOY TODAY. PEOPLE WORKED THEM TO THE BONE, OFTEN BEAT THEM, AND ONLY FED THEM SCRAPS.

Can a dog really be your best friend? No doubt. In the early 1900s, a large group of kids wrote essays about pets. Here's what they said about their dogs: he likes me, he guards me, he protects me, he barks when I come home from school, he's good to me. Notice how they use the word *he* as if the dog were a person? The kids also said that their dogs gave them love and affection by jumping up, running around, and playing with them. What's more, many said that their dogs hung out with them and played with them when they were feeling lonely or sad. And that's not all. What many people appreciate about dogs is that dogs love and accept them no matter what. Since canines can't speak, they never dish out advice, judgment, or criticism. They listen, but they don't tell your secrets. Studies show that dogs can change their owners' lives by making them happier, lowering their blood pressure, and helping them make friends by meeting other dogs and *their* owners. Talk about a best friend!

THE CAT

According to veterinary researcher Nicholas Dodman, a cat is like a miniature tiger in your living room. If a house cat goes AWOL, it can survive in the wild. Maybe that's because cats are born to hunt.

Check out the tracks this furry feline has made around the world.

Caracal

Wildcat

Sandcat

MUG SHOT

Names: Kitty, pussycat, "tomcat" for males, "queen" for females, and "kitten" for young cats

Domestication Date: About 9,500 years ago

Number in the World Today: Around 400 million

In the Wild: African, European, and Asian wildcats. Many domestic cats are also feral. They survive on their own in the wild.

Claim to Fame: No other animal has been so closely linked to superstition and magic.

People weren't the only mummies in ancient Egypt. Cat owners made cat mummies like this one when their pet cats died.

A Furry Mousetrap

What's up, pussycat? Mice and rats! That's what! Wherever mice and rats go, cats are sure to follow. This was no different in ancient Egypt thousands of years ago. As Egyptian farmers began storing grain in silos, or huge towers, mice and rats arrived in droves in search of a free lunch. And cats, most likely African wildcats, showed up hot on the heels of their favorite rodent "meals." The farmers were none too pleased to see the vermin gobble up their precious grain. So it wasn't long before the farmers welcomed cats as "micebusters" extraordinaire and even gave them the run of the place. The farmers began leaving out scraps of meat to attract the cats and soon realized that the cats also provided protection from poisonous snakes that were tailing the rats and mice for a tasty meal. In return, the ancient Egyptians gave the felines a home. And the cats soon became cuddly pets for people to love. In fact, when a pet cat died, ancient Egyptians shaved off their eyebrows to show they were in mourning. No wonder pet cats eventually spread from Egypt to households all over the world.

A corn snake (below, right) swallows a mouse whole. How's that for a gobsmacking meal?

Gotcha! Ha! Ha!

Ever seen a cat play with a mouse? Sometimes, cats will catch a mouse in their jaws, without killing the rodent, and then bat it around with their paws. Comical scenes like these between the hunter and the hunted may have inspired some of the world's first cartoons. Ancient Egyptian workers sketched and doodled humorous pictures of cats and mice on scraps of limestone and papyrus. What's more, these ancient doodles were much like *Tom and Jerry* cartoons, where Jerry the mouse always outwits Tom the cat. In the pictures, the Egyptians often reversed the natural order of things for comic effect. For example, one shows a kinglike mouse being waited on by cats and another shows a fierce army of mice attacking a castle of cats. And so cats and mice gave the world a good laugh and helped create cartoons, which continue to tickle the world's funny bone today.

No matter whether cats are big or small, they're hunters that stalk and pounce on prey for dinner. Gotcha!

In 945, cats were "guardians of the king's granary" in Wales. A cat was worth a penny at birth and four pennies after a mouse kill. Laws punished people for stealing or killing felines and these laws lasted for hundreds of years.

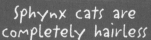

Sphynx cats are completely hairless

SPEAK OF THE BEAST

SHE LET THE CAT OUT OF THE BAG.

SHE GAVE AWAY THE SECRET. THIS SAYING MAY COME FROM A TRICK FARMERS PLAYED AT MARKETS HUNDREDS OF YEARS AGO: PUTTING A STRAY CAT IN A BAG AND SELLING IT AS A PIGLET. ONCE A CUSTOMER OPENED THE BAG, SHE DISCOVERED THE RUSE AND "LET THE CAT OUT OF THE BAG."

THE GUINEA PIG

Forget rats, mice, gerbils, and hamsters. Guinea pigs just may be the most popular pet rodent of all time.

Check out how guinea pigs have gnawed their way into people's hearts and given the world lots to chew on.

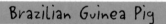
Brazilian Guinea Pig

MUG SHOT

Names: Cavy, pig, coney

Domestication Date: More than 3,000 years ago

Number in the World Today: Unknown

In the Wild: Brazilian guinea pig, shiny guinea pig, montane guinea pig, greater guinea pig

Claim to Fame: Guinea pigs have supplied lab results that led to 23 Nobel Prizes for medicine and physiology, the study of living organisms.

I Want My Guinea Pig

Guinea pigs roasting on an open fire in Ecuador

In the 1500s, guinea pigs became all the rage after Spanish invaders stumbled upon them in South America. The Inca, the people of the Andes, had been keeping guinea pigs as livestock as far back as 7000 BCE. The soft furry rodents lived with the Inca much like they live among rural South American families today. The creatures hung out in cages in Inca kitchens and wandered around their homes, munching on table scraps, until they were fat enough to be cooked for a delicious meal. They grunted when they seemed hungry, murmured when they seemed content, and squealed when they seemed afraid. Nevertheless, they rarely bit people. So the Spanish and other European sailors began bringing them home for their children as pets. England, in particular, went nuts for the rodents. Queen Elizabeth I had a pet guinea pig and so did many ladies of the Court. In fact, servants accompanied the ladies to and fro, carrying their guinea pigs on silk pillows.

Guinea pigs were a royal pain, er, pet in the court of Queen Elizabeth I.

Some guinea pigs bred for lab research have almost no hair and look like miniature hippos.

FACT TRACK

Guinea pigs have an immune system for fighting diseases similar to that of humans.

INTO THE LAB

Small, easy to care for, and easy to control. Not only did these characteristics make guinea pigs perfect pets, but they also made them perfect lab animals. What's more, guinea pigs didn't have a reputation for being dirty animals, like rats (see page 72). In 1780, a French chemist used guinea pigs in the lab to measure how much oxygen is used and carbon dioxide is produced during breathing. It wasn't the first time animals had been used in experiments. As early as the 100s, Roman doctor Claudius Galen experimented on pigs and apes to show that veins carry blood, not air. By the 1880s, guinea pigs were scurrying around lab cages all over Europe. In Germany, Robert Koch used furry little rodents to show that germs—a.k.a. microbes, or tiny microscopic organisms, that had just been discovered back then—spread diseases. Koch's experiments with guinea pigs went on to change the world by discovering a cure for the lethal disease TB, or tuberculosis, that was killing many people.

Guinea Pigs Crack the Case

Since guinea pigs were popular both as pets and lab animals, they often came up in debates over experimenting on animals. Around 1907, the side for experimenting on animals got a boost in public opinion when guinea pigs helped crack the mysterious medical case of scurvy. Back then, doctors didn't know the cause of the disease that results in swollen, bleeding gums and opens up old wounds. Nor did they have a reliable cure. However, experiments on guinea pigs showed that scurvy is caused by a poor diet. The lab rodents also showed that eating fresh fruit and vegetables prevents scurvy and that fruits and vegetables contain vitamin C, which neither humans nor guinea pigs can make in their bodies. Scientists then created synthetic vitamin C and tested it on guinea pigs. The experiments revealed that vitamin C keeps scurvy at bay. And so vitamin C pills popped into the world.

SPEAK OF THE BEAST

WILL YOU BE MY GUINEA PIG?

CAN I TEST SOMETHING OUT ON YOU? IN THE EARLY 1900S, AFTER GUINEA PIGS HAD BECOME POPULAR LAB ANIMALS, PEOPLE BEGAN CALLING A PERSON OR THING USED IN AN EXPERIMENT A "GUINEA PIG."

ANIMALS DID WHAT?!

CATS BEAT BACK THE EGYPTIAN ARMY

Egyptian goddess Bastet

Legend has it that the ancient Egyptians once won a war by sending thousands of cats into battle. As soon as the ferocious felines pounced on the enemy, the soldiers supposedly panicked and fled. Well, maybe this legend tells more about the power that the ancient Egyptians saw in cats than about the actual battle. History tells of another battle, though, in which cats beat back the Egyptian army.

According to Macedonian writer Polyaenus, in the Battle of Pelusium in 525 BCE, the Persian army painted cats on their shields and unleashed cats in front of the front lines. Once the Egyptians saw the cats in the ranks of their enemies, they ran for cover and the Persian army won.

The cunning strategy worked because the Egyptians thought cats embodied the Egyptian goddess Bastet, who had the body of a woman and the head of a cat. In fact, the Egyptians honored cats so highly that the punishment for killing one was death. So rather than fight the Persian army of cats, the Egyptians surrendered on the spot. You might say the cat got their tongue and then some.

CHAPTER 3

Animal Mall of Fame

You know your local mall, where you and your friends may check out fashion magazines, comb stores for the latest must-have jeans, play games in the arcade, visit puppies at the pet store, and eat sushi, pizza, falafel, roti, or wonton noodle soup?

It's a global marketplace. Chances are your local mall has the latest fashions from Paris, or knockoffs anyway, spices from India, oil from Italy, electronics and stuffed animals made in China, sneakers made in Indonesia, Persian carpets, Swiss watches, and games, books, and magazines from all over the world.

But it wasn't always so. Thousands of years ago, there were no highways or means of transportation for people to get around on, let alone move goods. Fashion trends didn't sweep around the world because the average person didn't know what people in faraway lands were wearing or even doing. Check out how the thread of the silkworm wove the eastern and western civilizations of the world together and inspired a great age of exploration that led people to new lands and to trade goods, thoughts, and ideas.

Spices from India

35

THE SILKWORM

Silkworms have no backbone, move slowly, and are no longer than the palm of your hand. But don't let that fool you. These caterpillars, the larvae of the silkworm moth, have inched their way through the world and cut a road longer than any other.

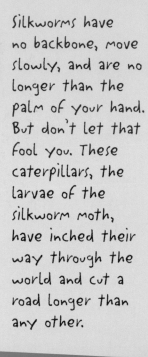

Silkworm cocoon

Mulberry leaves

MUG SHOT

Names: *Bombyx mori*, mulberry silk moth, silk moth caterpillar, test-tube caterpillar
Domestication Date: Around 3000 BCE
Number in the World Today: About 1 trillion, depending upon the season
In the Wild: None. Through domestication, the silkworm moth has lost the ability to fly.
Claim to Fame: Spins a cocoon that contains as many as 2 kilometers (1.2 miles) of silk strand

A Silkworm Drops In for Tea

Waiter, there's a worm in my tea! Maybe that's what Chinese empress Hsi-ling-shi said nearly 5,000 years ago when she picked some cocoons off a mulberry tree. She dropped one into her tea and a silkworm popped out. Ew! According to ancient legends, when the 14-year-old empress fished out the cocoon, it completely unraveled. She discovered it was one long, continuous strand, wrapped it around her finger, and thought she could make it into a beautiful cloth. Eventually, she did just that, and silk spun into the world. The fine, strong fabric had a unique soft glow that caught people's eyes and became highly prized. Legends say that the empress's husband began domesticating silkworms and developing methods to collect the silk thread from their cocoons.

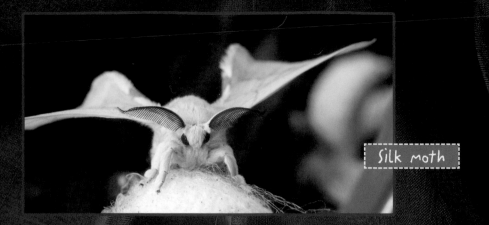

Silk moth

Trade Secret: Silk of Worm Ilk

Around 2700 BCE, the Chinese had thousands of silkworms on the job working around the clock to make silk. No joke! To make 1 kilogram (3 pounds) of silk, it takes thousands of cocoons and hundreds of thousands of mulberry leaves. The Chinese began the process by keeping and raising silkworm moths, which are native to China. The moths laid eggs on the leaves of mulberry bushes. Tiny worms hatched from the eggs. The worms gorged themselves on the mulberry leaves for six weeks straight, growing bigger and getting fat. Then these critters started spinning cocoons around themselves by oozing streams of liquid from their mouths that became solid fibers on contact with air. The Chinese fiercely guarded the secret of making silk for thousands of years. Demand for the shimmery cloth grew, and the Chinese grew rich supplying the demand. Roads sprang up for traders to carry silk to markets all over the world.

SPEAK
OF THE
BEAST

HE WORMED HIS WAY INTO THE GANG.
HE SLID HIS WAY INTO THE GANG, WITHOUT THEM REALIZING HE WAS DECEIVING THEM. THE TERM WORMED COMES FROM THE WAY WORMS MOVE, TWISTING ONE WAY THEN THE OTHER RATHER THAN MOVING DIRECTLY IN A STRAIGHT LINE.

The Road to All Markets

Eventually, the Silk Road wound its way to India, Persia, and Europe. Around 200 CE, the Silk Road was the longest road on Earth. It stretched some 6,400 kilometers (4,000 miles) across China to the Mediterranean Sea, linking the East with the West. Caravans of traders carried silk on camelback from China to India and Rome and brought wool, gold, and silver to China. And this exchange, started by the fabric of the lowly silkworm, changed the world as people began to trade, communicate, and share knowledge far and wide like never before. Other fabrics, rare dog breeds, recipes, spices, oils, medicines, furs, fireworks, precious gems, germs, human genes (biological material passed from parents to children that determines characteristics), diseases, and even art and religion began to flow along the road too. So did ideas and inventions. Some of China's greatest inventions—paper, printing, gunpowder, and the compass—reached the West via the Silk Road. And the spread of these inventions changed the world by allowing people to exchange stories, ideas, and maps through books (including the very book you are reading), newspapers, and magazines, fight with guns, and navigate through unknown territory. How's that for opening up a great age of exploration?

Chinese compass

To market, to market with silk fabrics and spices.

THE CODFISH

Rock cod

Bandits, robbers, and armies at war: all these dangers and more lay in wait for traders on the Silk Road. Sometimes the route was so dangerous to travel that parts were closed altogether. So in the 1400s, Europeans began to look for another route to China. They sailed west and landed smack-dab on the coast of North America. There were no silkworms or spices in sight, but there were zillions of codfish.

MUG SHOT

Names: Rock cod, scrod, northern cod, *morue franche, morue commune, morue de l'Atlantique,* ovak, uugak

Domestication: An attempt is under way to raise cod on fish farms.

Number in the World Today: Endangered

In the Wild: Atlantic cod, Pacific cod

Claim to Fame: Swims with its mouth open eating anything in its path, including Styrofoam cups, dentures, and young cod

FACT TRACK

The Chinese invented fish farming about 3,000 years ago. They kept carp in ponds and fed the fish waste from silkworms.

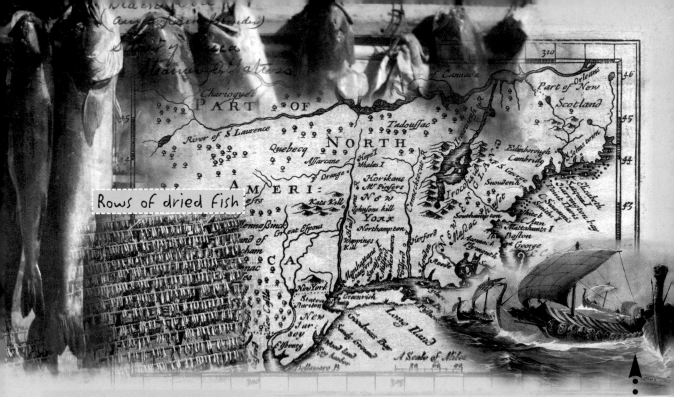

Rows of dried fish

LAND—ER, FISH—HO!

With visions of silk and spices dancing in his head, Giovanni Caboto, a.k.a. John Cabot, set sail from England in 1497. The Italian merchant sailed west across the Atlantic Ocean in search of a new route to China. He and his crew landed on the shores of a "new found land," where codfish were so plentiful they could scoop them up by the bucketful. Cabot mapped the new land, and the scads of cod soon drew fishers from all over Europe. Europeans couldn't seem to get enough fish, and Atlantic cod became their first choice. The result? The fishery was born in Newfoundland and cod flooded markets everywhere.

Have Cod, Will Travel

Cabot wasn't the first European to discover the bounty of cod on the Grand Banks. As early as 1000, the Vikings packed their long boats with dried cod, a nutritious food that wouldn't spoil on long voyages. The Vikings sailed west from Iceland and Greenland, and the dried stash helped fortify them all the way to the northern tip of the Rock—a.k.a. Newfoundland—the stomping grounds of the Atlantic cod, where the fierce seafarers could catch fresh fish for dinner.

What's more, researchers think the Basques of Spain and France may have also discovered the cod fishing grounds before Cabot. They think the Basques fished there in secret, salted and dried their catch, and then brought it to European markets. Salting cod before drying it makes the dried fish last even longer, and researchers think this allowed the Basques to sail even greater distances than the Vikings. Salt cod became a staple in European markets, and by 1550, more than half of all the fish eaten in Europe was cod.

41

Ever heard of Cape Cod? This outport on the eastern coast of the United States got its name from the huge schools of cod found there hundreds of years ago. In the 1600s, the cod lured boatloads of English settlers with the dream of making a living fishing in the British colony of New England. The settlers weren't very skilled at hunting or farming, so if they hadn't learned to fish cod, they might have starved. What's more, they only got good harvests once they learned to fertilize their farmland with cod waste.

Eventually, the settlers were catching more cod than they could trade with England. So they began trading hundreds of thousands of cod on the world market. They shipped cod to Spain in exchange for fruit, wine, coal, and iron. They shipped cod to the West Indies for sugar, molasses, tobacco, cotton, and salt. The British tried to limit this trading and that of other goods. They also barred New Englanders from the best cod fishing grounds and slapped hefty taxes on trade goods. This sparked the American Revolution. The settlers won the war and the United States of America was born. And so codfish helped change the map of the world.

ATLANTIC OCEAN

CAPE COD

TRURO VINEYARDS

CAPE COD BAY

SPEAK OF THE BEAST

THERE'S SOMETHING FISHY GOING ON.
SOMETHING CROOKED OR SUSPECT IS UNDER WAY. THIS EXPRESSION MAY COME FROM THE SMELL OF ROTTEN FISH.

Frozen Eats 'n' Treats

The next time you're at a grocery store, take a good look at all the frozen food. Much of it might not be there if it weren't for cod. Around 1915, Clarence Birdseye, a U.S. field naturalist working in Labrador, caught some cod that froze almost instantly in −40°Celsius (−40°Fahrenheit) weather. When he thawed it, he noticed that it tasted just like fresh fish, unlike the frozen seafood for sale in cities like New York. Birdseye discovered that flash-freezing fish stopped large ice crystals from forming in its cells as it froze so the fish wasn't damaged. He experimented with freezing fish fillets and invented a method to preserve the flavor and texture of fish. Frozen fish fingers, or fish sticks, made of cod soon followed. When they became available in grocery stores, they flew off the shelves. The world's appetite for cod rose and the era of frozen food began as frozen TV dinners, french fries, pizza, pizza pops, and Popsicles soon rolled off production lines into grocery stores everywhere.

Factory workers cut cod to make the frozen fillets people buy at grocery stores.

Cod Vanishes into Thin ...

Today, people chow down on cod in almost every country of the world. The fish is so popular that people have fished almost all the cod out of the sea. Cod is an endangered species, and fishing cod is banned in many fishing grounds. Some people are trying to raise cod in fish farms. If they are successful, the last food we catch in the wild may become domesticated, or tamed, on farms.

Factory worker packs cod on ice to keep it fresh.

A trawler fishing boat docks to unload its catch of cod.

THE BEAVER

Meet the largest rodent in North America. The beaver cuts down trees with sharp front teeth. It eats the bark and uses the branches to build dams and lodges, or homes, in water. Its fur is soft, shiny, and waterproof. Check out how the beaver changed the world, when European explorers, searching for a route to China, discovered the beaver in North America—and its fur became the hottest thing to wear.

MUG SHOT

Names: *Castor canadensis*, "kits" and "pups" for young beavers
Domestication Date: Beavers have not been domesticated.
Number in the World Today: 10 to 15 million
In the Wild: Beavers live in Canada, the United States, Norway, Poland, and Russia.
Claim to Fame: Beavers build dams and lodges in the water. They are hardworking builders that can replace an entire dam overnight.

The Beaver

44

Busy beavers bite the big one. No kidding! Beavers cut down trees with their teeth and use the trees to build dams.

Fashion Makes Fur Fly

In the Middle Ages, most Europeans didn't wear fur unless they were royals or nobles. Not only could they not afford to, but laws also banned common people from wearing fur. (Talk about fashion dos and don'ts!) Fur became a symbol of a person's position in society—a.k.a. a status symbol. Toward the end of the Middle Ages, this began to change as a middle class of society—bankers, lawyers, and merchants—made lots of money. They openly broke the "laws of fur." They bought what they wanted and wore what they wanted, such as hats made of sheared beaver fur, which became fashionable in the 1300s. In fact, these hats remained such a hot-ticket item for hundreds of years that beavers were almost wiped out in Europe and Russia.

45

BEAVERS OPEN UP NORTH AMERICA

In 1534, explorer Jacques Cartier shipped out from France to look for a northwest passage through the Arctic to China. Cartier and crew landed on the shores of Labrador and sailed to the Gulf of St. Lawrence. They met some First Nations people, traded knives for beaver pelts, and claimed the land for France. Word got out about the fine pelts and oodles of beaver there. French merchants sent a "search and capture" party to the St. Lawrence River to bring back beaver furs. Cartier didn't find a passage to China. But his expedition, and those of other explorers, slowly began to map and reveal the land of Canada.

Have to Have Hats

Around 1600, hats made of felt became all the rage in Europe. Everybody had to have one on his noggin. The fashionable hats had wide, stiff brims. Hatters made felt

Eager for Beaver

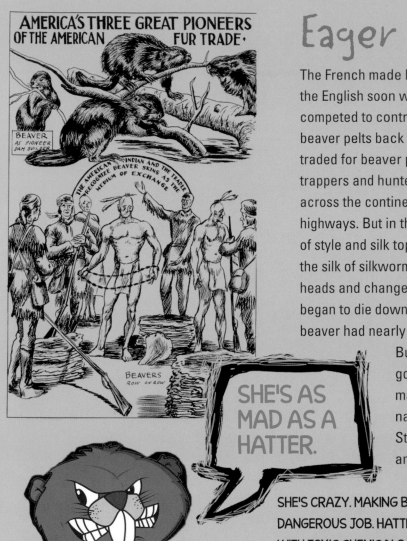

AMERICA'S THREE GREAT PIONEERS OF THE AMERICAN FUR TRADE·

BEAVER AS PIONEER DAM BUILDER

THE AMERICAN INDIAN AND THE TRADER RECOGNIZE BEAVER SKINS AS THE MEDIUM OF EXCHANGE

BEAVERS ROW ON ROW

The French made lots of money in the fur trade, and the English soon wanted a piece of it. The two rivals competed to control the land and sent shiploads of beaver pelts back to their countries. Both worked and traded for beaver pelts with First Nations people. As trappers and hunters caught beaver, they cut trails across the continent that later became railroads and highways. But in the 1800s, beaver felt hats went out of style and silk top hats from Paris came in. And so the silk of silkworms started popping up on people's heads and changed the world again. The fur trade began to die down—not a moment too soon, as the beaver had nearly become extinct in North America.

But the settlers did not pack up and go home. They found other ways of making a living and created the great nations of Canada and the United States. You might say they got busy and beavered away!

SHE'S AS MAD AS A HATTER.

SHE'S CRAZY. MAKING BEAVER FELT HATS WAS A DANGEROUS JOB. HATTERS TREATED BEAVER PELTS WITH TOXIC CHEMICALS THAT GAVE OFF POISONOUS FUMES. BREATHING IN THE FUMES COULD CAUSE BRAIN DAMAGE, AND SOME HATTERS EVEN WENT INSANE.

SPEAK OF THE BEAST

by pressing, heating, and treating hair from animal pelts with chemicals like mercury. And it just so happened that felt made of beaver pelts was one of the softest and smoothest kinds. To meet the demand for beaver fur, Russians went to Asia and eventually Alaska, and Europeans headed to Canada. The king of France charged explorer Samuel de Champlain with the task of developing the fur trade in Canada. Hunting beaver for the fur trade then drove the exploration, mapping, and settlement of North America for the next few hundred years as hunters, traders, and trappers hunted down the beaver in one area—and then moved to the next area to hunt more beaver.

Parthians ride into battle.

Silkworms Make the Romans Go Crazy

The Romans thought their eyes were playing tricks on them the first time they saw silk. The bizarre sight occurred in 54 BCE in a battle with the Parthians, the people who controlled what is now Iraq. The Parthians waved silk flags across the battlefield, and the strange material shone brightly in the sweltering heat of the desert sun, unlike anything the Romans had ever seen. It blinded them with fear!

But it wasn't long before the Romans were crazy for silk. They began paying huge sums of money to their enemies to get their hands on the stuff and fought many wars to control the Silk Road. The Chinese were so successful at keeping the origin of silk—a.k.a. the silkworms—a secret that all the Romans knew about the material was that it came from a land far, far away. Some even thought silk grew on trees.

Around 550 BCE, Roman emperor Justinian got fed up with constantly having to fork out for silk. He wanted his own stash. So he sent two monks to China to smuggle out the secret source. The monks stole some silkworm eggs and mulberry seeds. They hid them in hollow walking canes and brought them back to Rome. The bold move loosened China and Persia's stranglehold on the silk market. Silkworms and their wares spread through Europe and eventually wormed their way into the New World—modern-day North America.

CHAPTER 4

Animals at Work

Hey, Fido! Go fetch! Chances are, it didn't take our Stone Age ancestors long to put dogs to work once they domesticated them from wolves 15,000 years ago or so (see page 23). Take the *Qimmiq*, the Inuit name for the Canadian Inuit dog, for example. Some people think the hunting and sled dog is a pure breed some 10,000 years old. Others think the *Qimmiq* is the great-great-great-great-great-great-grandchild of wolves.

Whatever the case may be, the *Qimmiq* has done a ton of work in the Arctic. The big-boned, powerful dog has pulled sleds, sniffed out seals' breathing holes in ice for hunters, and held musk-ox and polar bears at bay to protect people. In 1909, the trusty sled dogs even helped Captain William Perry reach the North Pole.

Then there's the Labrador retriever that worked in fishing boats in the Labrador Sea off the coast of Newfoundland in the 1700s. The rugged, good-natured dogs helped pull in fishing nets, catch escapees from fishing lines, and retrieve fish that fell overboard.

Today, the Labrador retriever is one of the most popular pet dog breeds around. But people also breed dogs, such as German shepherds, for specific jobs, like police work. We also keep mutts at home with a mission—to sound a "bark-alarm" and scare any intruders away. And so work has gone to the dogs! Check out how pigeons, horses, camels, elephants, and dolphins have entered the workforce too and changed the world as we know it.

Canadian Inuit dog

Sled dog

Police dog

Horses

Elephants

49

PIGEONS

Sure, pigeons are plump with small heads and short, stubby legs. But that doesn't mean diddly-squat. The roly-poly birds are mean flying machines that can zoom through the air at more than 160 kilometers (100 miles) an hour for several hours at a time. Discover how pigeons have winged it around the world, changing history en route.

Spotted pigeon

Victoria crowned pigeon

Bleeding heart pigeon

Rock pigeon

MUG SHOT

Names: "Cock" for males, "hen" for females, "squab" for young ones under 30 days old, "fledgling" for young ones learning to fly, homing or carrier pigeon for messenger and racing pigeons, passenger pigeon for a wild species hunted to extinction

Domestication Date: About 5,000 to 10,000 years ago

Number in the World Today: 305 species. Due to human activity, numbers of some species have ballooned and others have shrunk.

In the Wild: 304 species live in the wild.

Claim to Fame: Flying more than 800 kilometers (500 miles) in a single day to find their way home from a place they have never been before

FACT TRACK

Splat! What's that? Ew! Pigeon droppings land everywhere. One pigeon alone poops 12 kilograms (26 pounds) of excrement a year. Good thing pigeon poop makes excellent fertilizer.

Where the Pigeons Fly

Say your friends played a trick on you. They blind-folded you and dropped you smack-dab in the middle of nowhere, a thousand kilometers away from home, in a place where you'd never been before. Could you find your way home without a compass or map? Could you take the shortest route? And could you go all the way without stopping to rest or refuel? No way? Well, a homing pigeon could and would. What's more, a homing pigeon could do it in about the same time as a car zooming down the highway at a speed of 95 kilometers (60 miles) an hour. Thousands of years ago, our ancestors recognized the unique homing ability of the squat birds and began taming and breeding them. Ancient Egyptians may have put pigeons to work first, releasing them in the four directions—north, south, east, and west—to deliver the message that a new pharaoh had risen to the throne. Egyptians also sent pigeons up and down the Nile River to relay messages about floods along the riverbanks.

In the wild, pigeons nest in coastal cliffs. Scientists think their homing ability comes from the birds' need to find food inland and return home. They think pigeons use the sun's position in the sky, the Earth's magnetic field, and visual landmarks to navigate. But even today scientists are not entirely sure how the zippy fliers do it.

SPEAK OF THE BEAST

PIGEONHOLED
TO PLACE SOMEONE IN A ROLE FROM WHICH THERE IS NO ESCAPE. THIS TERM COMES FROM A PIGEONHOLE—A SMALL NOOK IN A LOFT GIVEN TO A MESSENGER PIGEON TO ROOST.

The Pigeon Express

Before telegrams, FedEx, and texting appeared on the scene, pigeons were the world's fastest way to send a message. No joke! However many days a horse and rider took to deliver a message, a pigeon could do it in the same number of *hours*. People rolled up messages, stuffed them into tiny tubes tied to pigeons' legs, and released the birds to carry the messages home. Around 500 BCE, for example, the emperor of China had pigeons deliver messages from the provinces to Beijing. In 1150, the Sultan of Baghdad set up a pigeon postal service in his kingdom. In the 1200s, Genghis Khan created one that spanned Asia and much of eastern Europe. That way, as he invaded and took over new territories, he could send instructions to the capital to govern his expanding empire.

FLY AND DELIVER

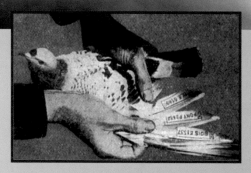

During World War I, pigeons carried coded messages.

Pigeons have even relayed news. In 776 BCE, the Greeks sent out the results of the first Olympic Games on the legs of pigeons. Each athlete brought a pigeon from his hometown and, if he won, released the bird to fly home with a message of his victory. In 51 BCE, Roman general Julius Caesar conquered Gaul and pigeons relayed the news to Rome.

By 1850, the telegraph system that sent messages lickety-split through wires had become the main means of communication everywhere. However, gaps among the wires still existed. So German businessman Julius Reuters used pigeons to close the gap between Brussels and Aachen. While a train took nearly eight hours to deliver news, stock market prices, and the like between the cities, pigeons got the job done in less than two. And so Reuters, now the world's largest news-gathering organization, flew into the world.

Agent 00-Pigeon

Sometimes the best spy for the mission is a pigeon. During both World Wars, soldiers couldn't always string telegraph wires across large battlefields. And even if they could, enemies could cut the wires or tap them to listen in. So soldiers often used pigeons to relay messages to headquarters from the field. In fact, during World War I, pigeons were the fastest and most reliable way to send a message. Some even carried tiny cameras on their chests to take surveillance photos as they flew over enemy territory. During World War II, submarines surfaced to release pigeons to deliver important messages. Pigeons were also dropped into enemy territory to collect information from civilians. One such feathered spy returned home with a message of more than 5,000 words and 15 map sketches of the location and movement of enemy troops. Others brought the location of an experimental bomb site in Germany. In the 1970s, the CIA made miniature cameras that weighed only as much as a few coins, strapped them to the chests of pigeons, and released the birds over enemy targets to take photos and return home. But just how that changed the CIA's view of the enemy targets is a mystery. To this day, details of these pigeon missions remain classified—a.k.a. top secret.

A soldier attaches a message to a carrier pigeon's leg.

A pilot releases a pigeon to send a message home.

During World War I, cages of pigeons were sometimes the only communication equipment on the battlefield.

HORSES

First, our Stone Age ancestors hunted wild horses for food and hides just like they did any other meaty, four-legged creature. But once they found they could get horses to carry heavy packs, train horses to pull carts, and "ride 'em, cowboy," the world was never the same. Giddy-up and get the scoop.

MUG SHOT

Names: "Stallion" for males, "mare" for females, and "foal" for young ones

Domestication Date: Around 5,500 years ago

Number in the World Today: About 58 million

In the Wild: Horses have been reintroduced into wildlife parks in Mongolia.

Claim to Fame: For nearly 5,500 years, before railways and cars roared onto the scene, horses were the fastest ride around.

FACT TRACK

In 1860, the Pony Express began delivering mail from St. Joseph to Sacramento via a relay of horse riders. A letter took 10 days to travel from city to city. The Pony Express was the fastest available message service until telegraph wires were strung 18 months later to send messages instantly, putting it out of business.

Ride 'Em, Steppe Boy!

Whoever threw a leg over a horse for the world's first ride had a lot of nerve. Horses are as unpredictable as creatures get. They can throw, buck, and toss riders into the dirt for no plain reason. No one knows who took the daring ride or where or when. But evidence shows that people in the steppes, or grassy plains, of modern-day Kazakhstan, had tame horses more than 5,000 years ago. Researchers think the people rode horses to hunt horses. Not only did riding horses give people a much faster way to get around than their own two legs, but it also helped them herd horses, as well as sheep and cattle. On horseback, a shepherd with a sheepdog can herd more than twice as many sheep as a shepherd on foot. So riding herders soon became wealthier than walking herders. Larger herds needed larger grazing areas and this may have sparked tribes to fight over territory. In turn, this may have led some tribes to make partnerships and others to make war. What's more, stealing horses and cattle—a.k.a. a tribe's wealth—got easier, as thieves on horseback could corral many at once and get away faster than thieves on foot.

THAT ENGINE IS 140 HORSEPOWER.

THE ENGINE HAS 140 UNITS OF HORSEPOWER. WHEN ENGINE-POWERED VEHICLES STARTED REPLACING HORSE-DRAWN VEHICLES, PEOPLE RATED THE VEHICLES IN UNITS OF HORSEPOWER. ONE UNIT OF HORSEPOWER EQUALS 550 FOOT-POUNDS PER SECOND. THAT'S ABOUT ONE-AND-ONE-THIRD TIMES THE ACTUAL POWER OF A HORSE.

SPEAK OF THE BEAST

Chariots

fortress on a hill

Alexander the Great

Horses Lead the Charge

Thousands of years ago, some of our ancient ancestors in the Near East, China, and Europe, began hooking up teams of horses to two-wheeled chariots. The horses changed warfare, charging into battle with a chariot, human driver, and archer in tow. Just the sight of them was enough to scare enemies silly, and with good reason. The horse-drawn vehicles aimed to crush as many enemy foot soldiers as possible, and the archers onboard aimed to slay the rest. In 1674 BCE, the Hyksos barreled into Egypt on chariots and routed the Egyptian army, taking over the entire country. At the time, the Egyptians had no chariots. Since the beast-led carts could carry soldiers into place much faster than foot soldiers—sometimes even before enemy troops knew they were there—the Hyskos had the edge. However, chariots ran amok on hills. So as armies began amassing horses and chariots, people began building fortresses on hills as a defense against the hoofed war machines.

HORSES = SPECIAL FORCES

The next step was to ride horses into battle. Enter the cavalry—a group of soldiers on horseback, wielding clubs or swords. The cavalry could attack swiftly, zip in where they wanted to, and exit out of danger quickly. Horse and rider functioned as a unit. They could charge over rough terrain better than chariots and change direction much more quickly and easily. Around 690 BCE, the Scythians, some of the world's first skilled riders, mounted horses with bows and arrows and raided the grass-lands of Europe and Asia. Their nimbleness, horsemanship, and ferocity surprised, frightened, and destroyed many neighbors. The Scythian cavalry formed a wedge, or triangle, shape to pierce enemy lines. They sacked rulers left and right and founded a powerful empire. Later, Alexander the Great, king of Macedonia from 336 to 323 BCE, learned the art of Scythian riding and used the wedge cavalry shape to conquer many enemies and build the largest empire in the world. And so horses changed the contest of war and the cavalry charged on until barbed wire and machine-gun fire cut them down in World War I and armored tanks all but replaced them in World War II.

A horse carries a cavalryman to battle.

Horses Run the Wild West

Wild horses couldn't drag cowboys, Native Americans, or anyone else to the Wild West before 1519. Horses had been extinct in North America for nearly 8,000 years until Spanish explorer Christopher Columbus brought some over with his expedition. Native Americans saw the edge horses gave the Spaniards and began to trade for the beasts right away. The whole way Native Americans hunted, traveled, and fought wars then changed as they began to do it all on horseback. The four-legged fleet runners became so valuable that those who had them had wealth and those that did not had naught.

Later, as European settlers arrived in North America, they brought more horses and hitched them to covered wagons. Then the horses pulled wagons loaded with the settlers and their possessions westward ho! In fact, horses provided most of the power settlers needed for transportation and plowing farms. And as cattle ranches sprung up in places like Texas, cowboys used horses to herd the cattle and drive the meaty creatures to railroads to market. Cavalry squads also protected new settlements from raids by "cowboys on the wrong side of the law." Some people say the Wild West couldn't have existed without horses.

Horses pulled wagons of settlers into the wild, Wild West.

CAMELS

They stink, they spit, and they bite. Nevertheless, camels have become some of the most prized animals on Earth. Check out how they've changed the world along the way.

Bactrian

Dromedary

Names: "Dromedary" for camels with one hump, "Bactrian" for camels with two humps, "bull" for males, "cow" for females, and "calf" for young ones.

Domestication Date: Camel dung found in Iran shows that the animals might have been domesticated more than 4,600 hundred years ago.

Number in the World Today: About 20 million.

In the Wild: No wild dromedaries exist today. Wild Bactrians are critically endangered and more rare than the giant panda.

Claim to Fame: Can travel up to 160 kilometers (100 miles) through the desert without drinking a drop of water.

Camels can crouch down and fold their legs under their bodies. Then the spittin' beasts are low enough for people to mount.

FACT TRACK

A dehydrated camel can drink about half a bathtub full of water in just one gulp.

58

Ships of the Desert

Ever wondered why camels are known as "ships of the desert"? Well, for starters, no animal can survive without food or water as long as a camel. Camels store fat in their humps that comes in handy as fuel when no food is around. The hairy beasts also have almost no sweat glands and excrete precious little water in their urine and dung. So they conserve water naturally. That's not all. Camels can withstand rising body temperatures that would kill most other mammals and have several unique adaptations that allow them to travel long distances through the desert. For example, two rows of long, thick eyelashes and an extra inner eyelid help keep blowing sand and grit out of their eyes. Their nostrils close almost completely to shut sand out. Thick pads on their feet help spread out their weight so they can walk on sand without sinking. What's more, camels can carry loads as heavy as 450 kilograms (990 pounds) as far as 47 kilometers (29 miles) in a day. And to top it all off, when people ride camels they may feel seasick, as camels rock from side to side. That's because camels walk by moving both the front and hind legs on one side of their body at once. It's enough to make you wanna hurl!

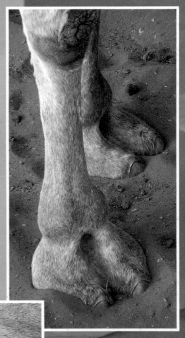

A camel's thick-soled feet don't sink in sand.

A camel's thick eyelashes bat away sand.

A camel's nostrils can close to shut out sand.

Today, people often ride camels just for fun.

Herding camels allowed people to survive where no human could before—in the desert, like present-day Saudi Arabia. People could live off the meat, milk, and wool of camel herds as they traveled from one desert oasis to another. What's more, camels were the perfect and perhaps the only animal that could survive in the wake of goat and cattle herds that ate up all the vegetation in areas, turning field into desert (see page 11), and take people along for the ride. Traders also loaded up camels with silk, spices, incense, and other goods and led camel caravans across long desert stretches, carving out the Silk Road and other ancient trade routes (see page 39). Not only did camel caravans change the world by moving goods from one place to another, they also helped spread ideas and religions, like Islam. Today, camels still transport almost one-third of the cargo that crosses the Gobi Desert in Asia and salt out of mines in Mali, Africa.

FACT TRACK

In the Gulf War of 1990–91 and the Iraq War of 2003, camels carried radio equipment and batteries in special harnesses so soldiers could communicate in remote desert areas.

60

ARMY STUNG BY DUNG

Australian Imperial Camel Corps

Fresh camel dung can light up your life. No joke! Camel poop is extremely dry and can be burned as fuel. During World War I, Allied soldiers in the Imperial Camel Corps (ICC) carried camel dung on the road as fuel to light fires. One time, they even used the poop to fool the Turks. First, the soldiers rode their camels in circles to make lots of tracks in the desert sand. Then they added extra piles of dung to the beasts' droppings to make it look as if they had three or four times the number of camels. The ruse seemed to work. The Turks shifted lots of troops from the front line to cover the ICC. This weakened their front line and Allied troops broke through it, leading the Turks to call for a truce. How's that for a secret weapon that created a big stink?

U.S. Camel Corps 1857

SPEAK OF THE BEAST

THE STRAW THAT BREAKS THE CAMEL'S BACK

YOU CAN ONLY PILE ON, OR DO, SO MUCH BEFORE A TINY INCREASE IN WEIGHT OR EFFORT TRIGGERS A COLLAPSE. PEOPLE USED SAYINGS LIKE THIS IN MANY LANGUAGES AS FAR BACK AS THE 1600S.

ELEPHANTS

Asian elephant

African elephant

Training and handling elephants is a dangerous job. The average elephant isn't easy to control, and working elephants have been known to haul off and kill their handlers without warning. But none of that has stopped humans from putting the giant beasts to work.

MUG SHOT

Names: "Bull" for males, "cow" for females, and "calf" for young ones

Domestication Date: Elephants have never been domesticated. Remember the sheep on page 14 who had their brains shrink, legs get shorter, and horns disappear as they were domesticated? Animals develop physical characteristics like these that are different from their wild ancestors as they become domesticated. Although people capture elephants and put them to work, these elephants are not different from their wild ancestors, like domestic animals are.

Number in the World Today: Between 508,000 and 743,000
In the Wild: Asian elephant and African elephant
Claim to Fame: The African elephant is the world's largest land animal. A male can stand twice as tall as the tallest basketball players and weigh more than two pickup trucks put together.

ELEPHANTS WORK AND BEAR IT

Meet the world's top beast of burden. A working elephant can carry a load as heavy as 500 kilograms (1,000 pounds) with its trunk for short distances and on its back for long distances. That's more weight than any other pack animal can bear.

Elephants can also do the job of a tow truck. No kidding! Before trucks and tractors were around, people used the wrinkly-skinned heavy lifters to pull wagons. And once motor vehicles putt-putted into the world, elephants sometimes bailed them out of roadside emergencies. According to World War I "elephant adviser" J.H. Williams, when trucks got stuck in the mud in the jungles of Burma (modern-day Myanmar), elephants pulled them out like "champagne corks out of bottles." Ta da! Elephants also built bridges in Burma. They dragged huge logs and maneuvered them into place with their trunks so soldiers could cross rivers safely. In fact, elephants kept the teak industry afloat in Burma. Before the war, about 6,000 floppy-eared lumberjacks hauled down teak logs cut high up in the forest. Just call them E-Haul!

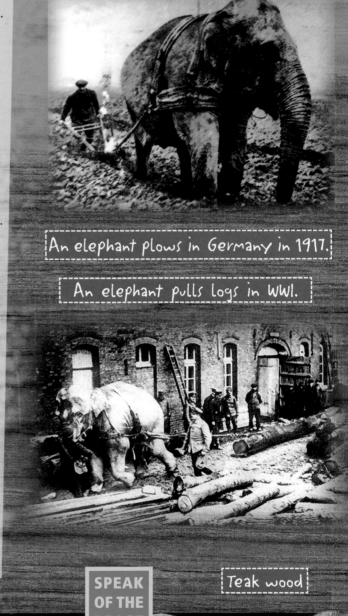

An elephant plows in Germany in 1917.

An elephant pulls logs in WWI.

Teak wood

SPEAK OF THE BEAST

YOU'VE GOT A MEMORY LIKE AN ELEPHANT.

YOU DON'T FORGET. THE SAYING AN ELEPHANT NEVER FORGETS MAY COME FROM THE FACT THAT WORKING ELEPHANTS REMEMBER MANY COMMANDS AND PEOPLE. AS WELL, SINCE ELEPHANTS LIVE FOR 50 OR 60 YEARS, THEIR MEMORIES LAST A LONG TIME.

Living Tanks Move Out

Bags, ammunition, rations, heavy equipment, and cannons: elephants can haul them all in the line of duty, take a bunch of soldiers for a ride, and also function as weapons to be reckoned with. In ancient times and as late as the 1800s in Southeast Asia, armies rolled out elephants like living tanks. They used elephants to trample enemy foot soldiers into the dust, to lift up horse and riders with their trunks and smash them to the ground, and to break down castle gates, walls, and towers like live battering rams. Some gates were even built to prevent elephants from bashing them at high speeds. Armies also used the thick-skinned creatures as psychological weapons. If soldiers had never tangled with elephants before, for example, they were likely to flee at first sight of the huge beasts of war. And once commanders had seen elephants in action, they thought twice about attacking enemies that had an elephant corps. Some battles were won

and lost by elephants. Sometimes, their sheer muscle power and the fear factor they evoked gave armies the winning edge. Other times, the use of elephants backfired, as loud noises or the killing of elephant handlers made elephants panic and retreat, crushing soldiers on their own side and sending troops into total chaos. The fact is, war elephants took a long time to train and remained tough to control, dangerous to use, and very unpredictable. And so artificial weapons and motorized tanks eventually replaced them.

FACT TRACK

Every year, a festival in Thailand pits one elephant against 100 men in a tug-of-war contest. The elephant usually wins!

FACT TRACK

Elephants can have violent mood swings. In circuses and zoos, elephants kill more handlers and keepers than any other animal.

ENDANGERED POSTER BEAST

Poof goes the elephant! Believe it or not, the big beasts have been vanishing off the face of Earth for nearly 2,000 years. As early as 77 CE, Roman politician Pliny the Elder noticed that African elephants were disappearing as people killed the magnificent creatures for the ivory of their tusks. Back then, ivory was all the rage in the Roman Empire and used extravagantly. The emperor Caligula had a stable made of ivory for his favorite racehorse! Around 400 CE, Themistius, a politician of Constantinople, predicted the herds would be eliminated from North Africa. And he was right. Around 700 CE, no elephants were left in Africa north of the Sahara Desert. Nevertheless, people continued to slaughter the creatures for ivory. In the late 1800s, demand for ivory hit another peak as people couldn't get enough jewelry, buttons, billiard balls, and piano keys made from the tough, lustrous stuff. In 1975, elephants appeared on the list of endangered species. Today, it is illegal to hunt elephants. But the demand for ivory hasn't died and poachers still shoot them to bag their tusks. Once a symbol of power, elephants now stand for endangered species all over the world. And so the poster beast continues to change the world by helping to raise awareness of how human activity can wipe out entire species.

Ivory tusks

Ivory dominoes and ivory piano keys

65

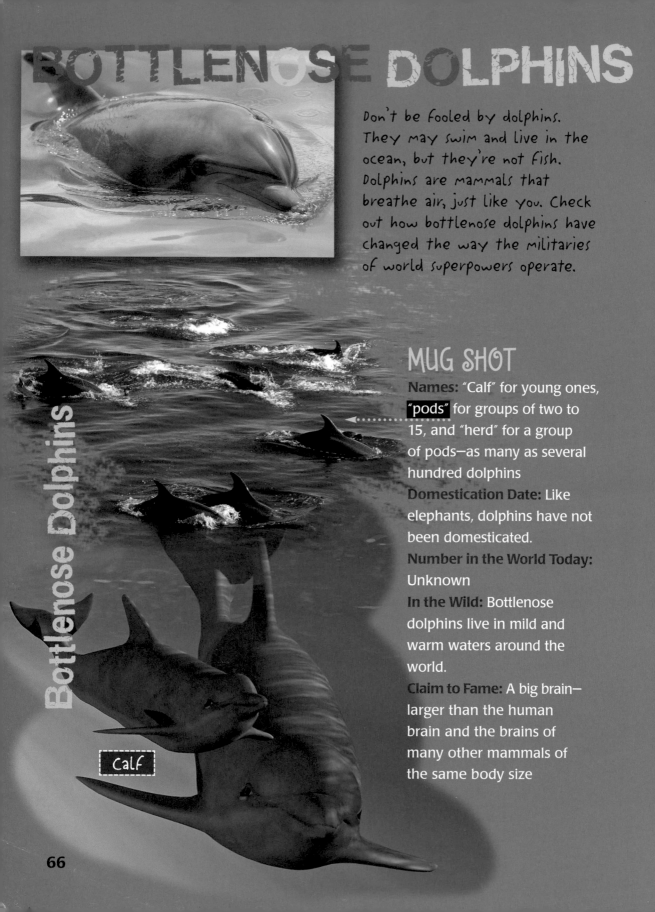

BOTTLENOSE DOLPHINS

Don't be fooled by dolphins. They may swim and live in the ocean, but they're not fish. Dolphins are mammals that breathe air, just like you. Check out how bottlenose dolphins have changed the way the militaries of world superpowers operate.

Bottlenose Dolphins

Calf

MUG SHOT

Names: "Calf" for young ones, "pods" for groups of two to 15, and "herd" for a group of pods—as many as several hundred dolphins

Domestication Date: Like elephants, dolphins have not been domesticated.

Number in the World Today: Unknown

In the Wild: Bottlenose dolphins live in mild and warm waters around the world.

Claim to Fame: A big brain—larger than the human brain and the brains of many other mammals of the same body size

Underwater Detectives

As the U.S. Navy sailed toward the Iraqi port of Umm Qasr during the 2003 Iraq War, two bottlenose dolphins dove deep down into the ocean to search for sea mines, explosive devices set to sink and destroy enemy ships. Sea mines detonate when a massive hunk of metal like a naval ship passes overhead. Ocean waves and bumps from animals do not set them off. Trained dolphins look for sea mines with echolocation, a natural form of sonar more sensitive than any developed by humans. They send out signal-like clicks and, when the clicks strike an object, they bounce back. This gives dolphins a mental picture of the object, including its size, shape, and speed! If the object looks like a mine, the dolphin swims to it and drops a marker, a weighted buoy line. The buoy floats to the surface, marking the location of the mine. Then the navy can send down divers to remove the mine or sail around it. The two dolphins above helped clear mines and give the navy a safe passage to Umm Qasr. What's more, some dolphins can even hold cameras in their mouths for underwater surveillance!

Attached to the dolphin's fin is a "pinger" device that allows the handler to keep track of the dolphin when out of sight. This dolphin is part of an operation to clear sea mines from shipping lanes.

Sea mine

A bottlenose dolphin surfaces while training to dive in search of mines.

Dolphins Report for Duty

In the 1950s, the United States started studying how dolphins swim to try to improve the design of submarines and torpedoes. U.S. military personnel soon realized that the marine mammals could be trained to patrol the sea around military operations and use their sonar to detect enemy swimmers that might be trying to plant bombs or wreak other havoc. That's not all. When the United States put them on security detail in Cam Ranh Bay during the Vietnam War, the dolphins also worked well as a deterrent. "In Cam Ranh Bay, they were getting weekly attacks with swimmers carrying explosives," a military official told the *Los Angeles Times* in 2009. Then the dolphins came on duty, "and they didn't have any attacks." But once the dolphins left the bay, the attacks started again. How's that for making the enemy blink and shift tactics?

Open wide! A handler brushes the teeth of a trained dolphin.

Come this way. Go back. Hand signals tell a trained dolphin what to do.

During the Cold War between the United States and the former Soviet Union (1945 to 1991) the two world superpowers used dolphins to guard their navy bases. What's more, they both admitted to it! Rumors surfaced that the superpowers also trained dolphins to seek and destroy enemy swimmers. The scuttlebutt said that U.S. dolphins were trained to shoot up enemies with a needle full of lethal carbon dioxide and Soviet dolphins knew how to stick mines onto enemy ships and balls of carbon dioxide onto divers. However, neither the United States nor the Soviets has admitted to giving dolphins any such licenses to kill. Today, the Soviet-trained dolphins work with children with mental illness, while a squadron of U.S.-trained dolphins provide security for the navy's Kings Bay submarine base in southeast Georgia. The base hopes the presence of this "dolphin marine corps" may put the kibosh on any terrorist attacks.

DOLPHINS FIGHT THE COLD WAR

SPEAK OF THE BEAST

HE HAD TO JUMP THROUGH HOOPS.

HE HAD TO DO A BUNCH OF DIFFICULT THINGS TO GET WHAT HE WANTED. THIS SAYING BRINGS TO MIND A PICTURE OF A PERFORMING ANIMAL—SUCH AS A DOLPHIN—DOING TRICKS FOR FOOD REWARDS.

PIGEON GETS PAST ENEMY FIRE

During World War I, a squad of American soldiers got trapped behind enemy lines. As if being surrounded by enemy soldiers wasn't bad enough, their own side didn't know they were there and began firing on them. The squad tried to send word of their predicament to their fellow soldiers. They wrote a message, rolled it up, and placed it in a tube tied to a messenger pigeon's leg. Then they released the bird. But German soldiers spotted the winged messenger and shot it down. The Americans sent out a second pigeon, and the Germans blasted it out of the sky too.

The squad had only one messenger pigeon left. Feeling desperate, the commander wrote the message, "We are along road 276.4. Our artillery is dropping a barrage directly on us. For heaven's sake, stop it," sealed it in the messenger's tube, and let the pigeon go.

As the bird flew up, the Germans opened fire. A stream of bullets whizzed all around the pigeon. One bullet pierced it in the breastbone and the bird began to drop. Another blinded it in one eye and another hit one leg. But nothing could stop the pigeon. The wounded bird made it all the way home with the message intact. The Americans stopped firing on their own troops and, within hours, the survivors of the squad were safely behind American lines.

Here's a photo of the message the wounded pigeon delivered through enemy lines.

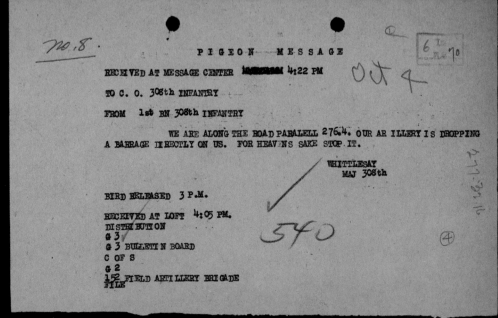

no. 8.

PIGEON MESSAGE

RECEIVED AT MESSAGE CENTER 4:22 PM

TO C. O. 308th INFANTRY

FROM 1st BN 308th INFANTRY

WE ARE ALONG THE ROAD PARALELL 276.4. OUR ARTILLERY IS DROPPING A BARRAGE DIRECTLY ON US. FOR HEAVENS SAKE STOP IT.

WHITTLESAY
MAJ 308th

BIRD RELEASED 3 P.M.

RECEIVED AT LOFT 4:05 PM.
DISTRIBUTION
G 3
G 3 BULLETIN BOARD
C OF S
G 2
152 FIELD ARTILLERY BRIGADE
FILE

CHAPTER 5

Secret Agents of Disease

Ever seen secret agents in action in the movies? Some animals are a lot like them. They go about the world doing "dirty work" undercover. They sneak onto ships and creep into sacks and stow themselves away so people are none the wiser. Then they travel around the world, making "special deliveries" at each and every stop where they arrive.

Many operate for others, just like secret agents operate for countries. What's more, many are like sleeper agents who have no idea they're even on a mission. They just go about their daily business of living—searching for food, eating, and sleeping—unknowingly spreading diseases of mass destruction that kill people along the way.

Others kill as they seek to take over territory and replicate, or reproduce themselves. They learn about the defenses of their foes and then evolve new versions, or generations, of themselves to outwit them. Find out who some of them are and how close they have come to taking over the world.

SPECIAL DELIVERY
DISEASE

THE RAT

Whether you think they're warm and fuzzy critters or complete and filthy vermin, no animal has changed the world quite like the rat. Check it out.

MUG SHOT

Names: The brown rat is also called the Norway rat. The black rat is also called the ship rat, house rat, and roof rat.

Domestication Date: Around 300 years ago

Number in the World Today: Unknown

In the Wild: Rats live in the wild and almost everywhere people live.

Claim to Fame: Rats are **deadly** "sleeper agents." They have probably killed more people than any war or natural disaster in the world.

Pet rat

Newborn rats—the next generation of "sleeper agents"

Rats Colonize the World

Just call rats "accidental tourists"—tourists that come to stay, that is. They don't migrate and they rarely wander more than 180 meters (200 yards) from their homes—houses, barns, silos, or ships—anywhere people have stored food or garbage that rats can gnaw on for a good meal. But they do enter sacks of grain and scurry up and down the ropes of docked ships. And if those sacks get shipped or those ships set sail, the rats will go along for the ride, sometimes traveling hundreds of kilometers away. That's how the black rats originally from southeastern Asia spread around the world.

Mounds of trash attract rats.

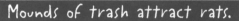

FACT TRACK

Some rats are fitter, faster, and stronger than ever before. New "super rats" that have evolved to resist rat poisons are infesting British towns and cities.

"Secret Agents" of Black Death

In the Middle Ages, between 1347 and 1351, black rats carrying fleas infected with the Black Death, or bubonic plague, carried the lethal disease along trade routes from Asia to Europe. Landing at trading posts and scampering ashore at ports, the rats spread the Black Death through Europe. The plague killed 25 million people—about one-third of the entire of population of Europe. Many people believed it was the end of the world. People were dying every-where they turned. Back then, no one knew that rats were spreading the disease or that fleas carrying *bacilli* bacteria, which causes the plague, had infected the rats. Once the Black Death snuffed out the rats, the fleas "jumped ship" for a new host—humans—injecting the lethal bacteria as they bit and fed on people. Swollen black spots called buboes then appeared on the people and most died soon after. Is it any wonder people were afraid?

Flea

PLAGUE

is passed to Man by WILD RODENTS, Rabbits, and by their FLEAS

an EASILY-CAUGHT Wild Animal is probably SICK

never handle them!

RESTRAIN YOUR PETS
they can carry infected fleas to you
USE Flea Powder on each pet

**Do NOT
pitch tents or lay**
Bedrolls on or near nests or burrows

Use Insect Repellants

SEE YOUR DOCTOR

about ANY unexplained illness

Plague is CURABLE
WHEN TREATED IN TIME

Rats scamper up and down the ropes of docked ships to board ships and go ahsore.

Rats! It's an Invasion

If you tune into news about the environment, chances are you've heard of "invading species." When these animals or plants not native to an area arrive, look out. They can virtually wipe out native animals or plants as they move in and proceed to take over, hence the name "invading species." Well, rats are one of the original and most destructive invaders. Around 400 CE, stowaway rats on the canoes of Polynesians landed in Hawaii. They invaded the underground burrows and habitats of crevice-nesting seabirds. The ravenous rats attacked the nesting colonies, eating eggs, chicks, and even adult birds. And so they had a big hand—er, claw—in the extinction of many seabirds. In fact, invading rats have taken over 90 percent of the world's islands and island chains this way, eliminating seabirds and also eating island reptiles, frogs, and plants into extinction. Experts say that by gobbling up fruits, seeds, and flowers, rats can alter forests and change the entire environment of islands. What's more, the voracious rodents likely remain the biggest threat to seabirds today.

SPEAK OF THE BEAST

DID SHE RAT ON YOU?

DID SHE TELL ON YOU OR BETRAY YOU? THIS EXPRESSION COMES FROM THE BELIEF THAT RATS ARE CUNNING CREATURES, READY TO DESERT SINKING SHIPS AT THE FIRST SIGN OF TROUBLE.

MOSQUITOES

Mosquitoes want to suck your blood. There are just no ifs, ands, or buts about it. Check out how the little buggers' appetite for blood has taken a huge bite out of the world.

Mosquito full of blood

Tiger mosquito

Mosquito larvae

MUG SHOT

Nicknames: Skeeter, bloodsucker

Domestication Date: Mosquitoes have been around for more than 79 million years and have never been domesticated.

Number in the World Today: About 3,000 different species

In the Wild: Mosquitoes live all over the world except for Antarctica and inner Greenland.

Claim to Fame: The number-one agent of disease in the animal kingdom

A Real Bloodsucker

Mosquitoes are like vampires. They come out between dusk and dawn, bite unsuspecting creatures to feed on blood, and have built-in sensors for finding victims. The tiny insects can sense the body heat of warm-blooded creatures and the chemicals of human sweat. They can also sense the carbon dioxide breathed out by animals or people who are more than one-third of a football field away. But only female mosquitoes are bloodsuckers. They gorge themselves on a meal of blood to lay eggs. If one lands on you, it'll prick your skin with a long, thin proboscis to suck your blood. And if you don't catch it in the act, or swat it away, it'll suck away until its entire tummy, or abdomen, is full. Its saliva "greases" your blood with proteins to stop your blood from clotting. That way, your blood is easier to suck. Later, the saliva makes your skin itchy. And sometimes, skeeter spit can be downright deadly—laced with a dose of a fatal disease such as malaria, yellow fever, or West Nile virus.

Proboscis

AGENTS IN ACTION

Mosquitoes aren't the animal kingdom's top agent of disease for nothing. The bloodsucking menaces do their dirty work using one of the oldest rules of war: know the enemy. As insecticides are developed to kill mosquitoes, mosquitoes "learn" about them and develop resistance to them. And the disease-causing microbes injected by mosquitoes also learn how to resist "treatment."

Who Killed Alexander the Great?

Alexander the Great in action

Alexander's empire

In 323 BCE, Alexander the Great (ATG) ruled the world. No army could beat the notorious warrior king in battle. Piece by piece, ATG had fought and won an empire bigger than anyone had ever commanded before. His empire stretched all the way from modern-day Greece to India, including parts of Egypt and North Africa to boot. So when ATG caught a fever sailing through the marshes of ancient Babylon and dropped dead two weeks later, the world was stunned.

ATG was in the prime of life, just 32 years old. What or who killed him, everyone wondered. In fact, people are still trying to solve the mystery today. Some say an enemy poisoned him. Others say heavy drinking did him in. Still others say a blind assassin bit him. *Say what?* In studying written records of the king's illness, modern researchers think a mosquito bite may have infected ATG with a deadly dose of malaria, yellow fever, or West Nile virus. Talk about biting the big one!

Grrr! Alexander the Grrreat busts out in a lion headdress.

FACT TRACK

Why does a mosquito bite swell up into an itchy red bump? The little bloodsucker's saliva triggers an allergic reaction in your body.

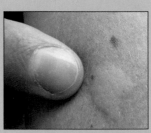

Killer Bites Shut Down Site

Ship in the Panama Canal

Panama Canal

Bzzz. Bzzz. In the late 1800s, a swarm of mosquitoes buzzed around the construction site of the Panama Canal, which workers were building to link the Atlantic and Pacific oceans. The bothersome bugs bit the workers, and the workers bit the dust left and right. Thud! Thud! No one had bug juice to repel mosquitoes back then. What's more, people didn't know that mosquitoes can carry killer diseases. When mosquitoes bite an infected bird and draw blood, for example, they may pick up disease-causing microbes or viruses in their spit, or saliva. Then as the skeeters bite other creatures and leave some spit behind as a "parting" gift or itch, mosquitoes blindly spread the microbes. This bite, or kiss of death, stopped the construction of the Panama Canal until mosquitoes were virtually eliminated from the area around 1912. Once built, the canal allowed ships to travel between the east and west coasts of the United States without having to sail all the way around South America, and trade began to skyrocket around the world. Today, ships carry cars, oil products, grains, and coal between Asia and the United States through the Panama Canal.

I'M SICK. IN EVERYDAY CONVERSATION, PEOPLE OFTEN CALL MICROORGANISMS THAT CAUSE THE FLU AND OTHER ILLNESSES, "BUGS." SO WHEN THEY GET SICK, THEY SAY THEY HAVE A BUG.

I'VE GOT A BUG.

SPEAK OF THE BEAST

RATS RUN RIOT

Long, long ago, when ancient Romans conquered Egypt, they brought cats home to Europe. But as any cat owner knows, cats are independent creatures that come and go as they please and stay out all night hunting under the dark cover of the night sky.

And maybe their stealthy nighttime operations did them in. For in the Middle Ages, cats fell under suspicion as Europeans looked at them with superstition. Many Europeans believed the slinky felines were evil witches in disguise, and they hunted down domestic cats in Europe almost to extinction.

Today, some people think that's why the Black Death hit Europe so hard, killing off millions of people. Since there were hardly any cats around to kill the infected rats, the rats ran rampant, carrying the plague along for the ride.

In 1908, a British scientist put this theory to the test during a plague outbreak in India. Using the logic that "cats kill rats,"

Dr. Buchanan did a census of cats in Indian villages. The doctor found that in villages where there was one cat or more for every two houses, there was no plague.

He also found that as the number of cats in an area rose, the number of plague cases fell. So who knows how cats might have changed world history if they had been around when the plague-infected rats scurried ashore in Europe? All we can say for sure is that "cats kill rats" and that is that.

CHAPTER 6

Animals in You

Quick! Think fast: What animal has changed the world the most? Would you say goats, dogs, rats, microbes, or none of the above? Have you noticed something peculiar about how all these animals have altered things? Namely, that they've all had help from a rather singular partner in time: none other than human beings—a.k.a. people like you and me?

The fact is that herds of goats might not have trampled and overgrazed land around the world if they hadn't been kept and put out to pasture by people. And dogs might never have evolved from wolves if wolves hadn't struck up a friendship with people (or was that the other way around—that people befriended wolves?). And rats? Well, rats might never have carried the microscopic bug of the Black Death that decimated Europe during the Middle Ages if they hadn't hitched a ride in the sacks of grain and ships that people were running along trade routes.

Maybe you don't think of yourself as an animal. Well, that's okay. Many people don't. Nevertheless, human beings, like all creatures on Earth, have evolved from animals that lived billions of years ago. And you are also home to millions of microbes that help you go about the business of living each and every day. Turn the page to meet some of the animals in you and find out how they've changed the world.

Rod-shaped microbes like the magnified purple ones you see here couch-surf in your gut 24/7.

Don't be shy. Let your gorilla out!

MICROBES

You can't see microbes with the naked eye because they're so tiny, but they're out there—here, there, and everywhere. They are in the soil, water, air, and even your very own body. Check out how microbes go to work in the world and change your world from the inside out.

MUG SHOT

Names: Bacterium, bug, germ, microscopic organism

Domestication Date: Around 100 years ago. People have developed microbes to make medicine, vaccines, vitamins, and foods like cheese and yogurt.

Number in the World Today: Way too many to count. Just the upper layer of dry soil has 10 million bacteria per gram.

In the Wild: Microbes are everywhere—even in your hair.

Claim to Fame: Microbes were the first forms of life on Earth.

MY PHONE HAS BEEN BUGGED!

SPEAK OF THE BEAST

A LISTENING DEVICE HAS BEEN PLANTED IN MY PHONE! IN EVERY-DAY CONVERSATION, PEOPLE CALL HIDDEN LISTENING DEVICES "BUGS" AFTER MICROBES, WHICH ARE INVISIBLE TO THE NAKED EYE.

FACT TRACK

You won't find microbes listed in the animal kingdom. Gone are the days when scientists classified all living things into two kingdoms—plants and animals. In studying microbes, scientists realized they are quite different from plants and animals and gave them their own kingdoms. How's that for ruling the world?

This Place Needs Some Atmosphere

Once microbes began to inhabit Earth, they made some serious changes. Oh sure, they took their time about it—about 1.5 billion years or so—but the tiny bugs changed the atmosphere of the place completely. No joke! As they evolved, they began to obtain energy from sunlight. Then they evolved further into bacteria that could photosynthesize—absorb sunlight and chemicals from the atmosphere to produce energy and oxygen. This broke new ground, leading to the development of green plants on Earth. And as more and more green plants took root and photosynthesized, they flooded the atmosphere with oxygen, which all animals and people depend upon today to breathe. Can you guess what happened next? That's right. Animals began to evolve on Earth, and eventually people evolved in their footsteps.

Life 1.0

No one knows how life began on Earth. Scientists think the Earth is about 4.6 billion years old. The planet had no oxygen back then. The sun blazed down on barren rocks and oceans with extreme heat. Volcanoes erupted and thunderstorms struck frequently. Over time, a chemical soup of the essential ingredients of life—fats, sugars, amino acids, and nucleic acids—built up in the oceans. Then about 3.5 billion years ago, the first form of life appeared in the oceans. Somehow, these conditions cooked up microbes—invisible organisms like bacteria that could survive without oxygen. And the world has never been the same since.

THE ZOO IN YOU

Your body is like a zoo for microbes. Trillions of the tiny bugs lounge around on your skin, and trillions more camp out inside your nose, mouth, throat, and gut. In fact, your body has 10 to 20 times more microbes than human cells. And scientists think you might not be able to live without them. The microbes that hang out in your gut, for example, eat whatever you eat. As they help themselves to your three square meals a day, they help you digest food and convert it into energy. That's energy you can use to think, dream, walk, run, dance, sing, skateboard, make stink bombs, scale mountains, and build rockets. Just think of all the people microbes have powered up through time to hunt down dinner, sail around the world, catch fish, plant crops, fight wars, build pyramids, construct bridges, make art, invent computers, and land on the Moon. How will your energy change the world? One thing's for sure: microbes can help give you the brainpower to imagine it.

Human digestive tract

Influenza virus

War of the Microbes?

Citizens of the world, beware—it's a microscopic jungle out there and, sometimes, even in there, right inside you!

Even before we discovered that microbes get under our skin and some can make us sick, we began to fight back. Our immune systems

Microbes Rot Flesh

Life wouldn't exist on Earth without microbes. That's because microbes are like the batteries that power up the "cycle of life." Here's how. They make the flesh of dead animals rot. No kidding! As organisms die, microbes in the soil break them down. This returns the nutrients in the organisms' bodies to the soil. Then plants can use these nutrients to grow and photosynthesize, taking up carbon dioxide from the atmosphere and releasing oxygen for animals and people to breathe. What's more, microbes are essential to the process of weathering and breaking down rocks to make soil. And without soil, there would be no plants, and without plants, there would be no grass for cows and other animals to eat. And without plants, cows, and other animals, there would be nothing for humans to eat. The whole world would go hungry and all life would die out!

O_2

CO_2

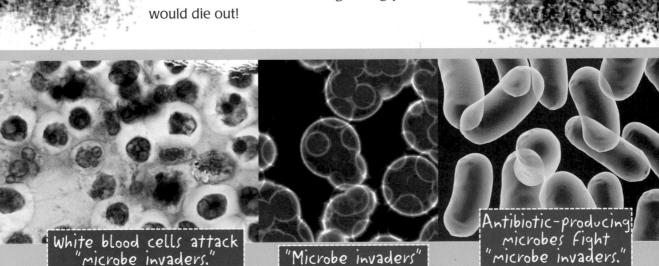

White blood cells attack "microbe invaders."

"Microbe invaders"

Antibiotic-producing microbes fight "microbe invaders."

flush out "microbe invaders" by engulfing them with white blood cells. We also develop fevers to "burn them out." But sometimes these human defenses work and sometimes they don't. The fact is that disease-causing microbes keep evolving to trick their way past our defenses. And humans keep evolving to outwit microbes and stay healthy and alive.

Humans have also devised a way to beat microbes with microbes. No joke! In the mid-1900s, scientists discovered antibiotics—chemicals produced by certain microbes that will kill other microbes without killing people or damaging human bodies. So now people take antibiotics to fight off and kill microbe invaders that stir up infections.

FISH

You are a fish out of water. No joke. Check out your "inner fish" and find out how fish changed the world by crawling out of the sea.

Clown Fish

Sushi

MUG SHOT

Names: Large groups of fish are called "schools."

Domestication Date: Most kinds raised on fish farms today were domesticated around 1900.

Number in the World Today: Unknown

In the Wild: Many fish still live in the oceans, but several have been hunted almost to extinction.

Claim to Fame: Fish are the last creatures people still hunt in the wild for food on a large scale.

Fish Invade Land

Fish gotta swim—and fish gotta crawl. That was the story on Earth more than 375 million years ago, when one fish went where no creature had gone before. The fish did a pushup on its fins and crawled out of the sea onto land. How do we know? In 2006, scientists found a fossil of a fish that had a flat head with eyes on top like a crocodile's head and arm bones like those of a shoulder, elbow, and wrist in its fins. The discovery made news headlines around the world, because these arm bones were a lot like those of ancient, primitive land-living creatures. Scientists named the fossil *Tiktaalik*, which means "large freshwater fish" in Inuktitut, the language of the Inuit on Ellesmere Island where the fossil turned up. Scientists think *Tiktaalik* was one of the first fish to invade land and that once fish did, they eventually evolved into all the land-living creatures we know today. Call it one small step for fish and one giant leap for creatures of all kinds.

Fish Fossil, China

Fish have landed.

Something's Fishy . . .

Ever heard the theory that what sets human beings apart from animals is our remarkable brainpower and our ability to walk on two legs, leaving our extremely agile hands free? Just say hello to your inner fish. The `backbone` that holds you up so you can walk on two legs first appeared in fish. Your head, which holds your brain in a helmetlike skull of bone along with all the wiring that your brain has to send and receive signals from your nerves, mouth, nose, eyes, and ears, also first evolved in fish. What's more, the bones in your arms that make up your shoulder, elbow, and wrist come courtesy of fish like *Tiktaalik*, mentioned on page 87. Who knew humans were so fishy?

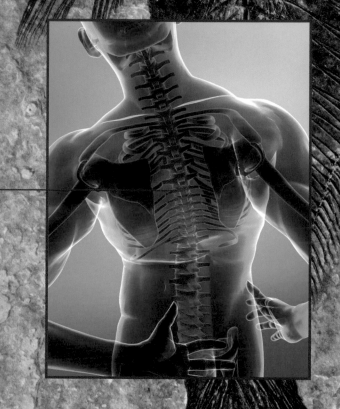

A COLD FISH

SPEAK OF THE BEAST

A PERSON NOT MOVED MUCH BY EMOTIONS. SINCE FISH ARE COLD-BLOODED RATHER THAN WARM-BLOODED LIKE PEOPLE, THEY'RE OFTEN BELIEVED TO BE COLD AND UNFEELING. HENCE, THE SAYING A COLD FISH BUBBLED UP.

It's a Fish-Eat-Fish World

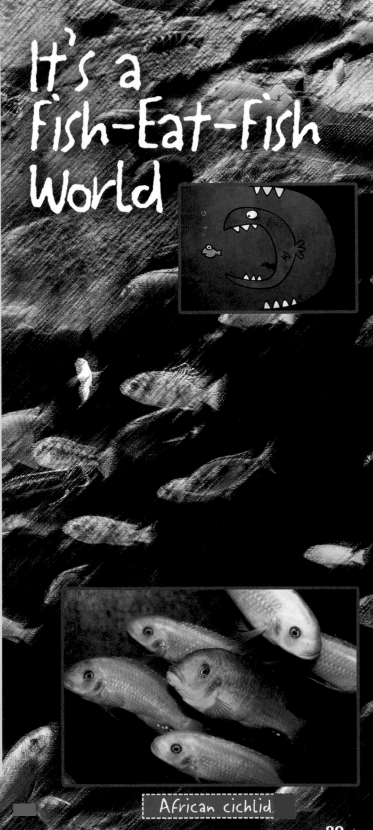

If reading all this hasn't left you feeling like a fish out of water, consider this: research shows that fish have some of the most complex social systems on Earth. Some fish have relationships among them that seem almost human. Sure, big fish eat little fish, even swallowing them whole—just as people sometimes feel that it's a "dog-eat-dog" world out there, where they must look out for their own interests or else. But researchers studying the social lives of African cichlids, colorful freshwater fish in Lake Tanganyika, have also found that fish help each other like people do. The researchers have observed the fish living together in groups of 10. One pair of the fish breed and the other fish appear to be helpers that look after the brood, defending the territory, cleaning the nest, and even giving the babies the fish equivalent of a bath. In exchange for their cooperation, the helper fish get a place to live and protection from predators. How's that for scratching and watching each other's backs?

African cichlid

Bigfoot Appears as the Missing Link

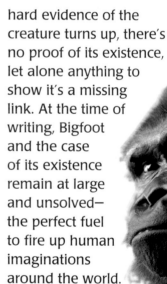

It's a man … it's an ape … it's Bigfoot! All around the world, people claim to have seen rare, massive, hairy, apelike creatures that walk like people. In Canada, people call the creature Sasquatch, an Aboriginal word for "wild man of the woods." In the mountains of the Himalayas, people call it Yeti, or the Abominable Snowman. In Australia, it goes by Yowie, in Russia, Alma or Wild Man, and, in China, Yeren or Man-Monkey.

Since scientists think that human beings evolved from apes, some people have even called Bigfoot the missing link between apes and humans, a creature with physical characteristics of each species. Others have said that Bigfoot is a surviving specimen of the largest ape that ever lived—*Gigantopithecus*—that beat its chest on Earth 500,000 years ago.

The only problem is that despite so many reported sightings, no bones or teeth of Bigfoot have ever been found. So many people think Bigfoot is just a myth. Until any hard evidence of the creature turns up, there's no proof of its existence, let alone anything to show it's a missing link. At the time of writing, Bigfoot and the case of its existence remain at large and unsolved—the perfect fuel to fire up human imaginations around the world.

Have you seen Bigfoot?

Ape

CHAPTER 7

Gecko Lizard

Animals Spark Inspiration

Albatross

What makes superheroes super? Their superhuman powers, right? You bet! But have you ever noticed that some of the world's favorite superheroes, like Spider-Man, Batman, and Wolverine, have characteristics or powers like those of animals? Or that the same is true of supervillains like Catwoman and the Penguin?

The fact is, animals can do many things that seem extraordinary to people but are just ordinary things in the everyday lives of the animals. A gecko lizard, for example, can defy gravity and walk upside down on a ceiling. A beaver can swim underwater for 15 minutes without coming up for air.

That's not all. A cheetah can sprint as fast as 100 kilometers (60 miles) an hour. An ant can lift 10 times its own body weight or more. An albatross can fly all around the world in 46 days. Is it any wonder animals have been the inspiration for superheroes that rule the pages of comic books and ignite the silver screen? Check out how animals have inspired art, fashion, inventions, and ideas that have changed the world as we know it.

Cheetah

91

BIRDS

About 100 years ago, flying was for the birds as far as people were concerned. But not for lack of trying. Check out how birds changed the world with the secret of flight.

King vulture

Kiwi

Magpie chicks

Names: Young birds are called "chicks." **Domestication Date:** Geese were kept by our Stone Age ancestors around 10,000 years ago.

Number in the World Today: More than 9,600 species **In the Wild:** Many species have never been domesticated. **Claim to Fame:** Birds are the only living creatures covered in feathers.

Peacock

So You Wanna Fly ...

Ever watched a bird soar through the sky and wished you could fly? You're not alone. People have wanted to wing it like birds for eons. About 17,000 years ago, some of our Stone Age ancestors made cave paintings at Lascaux that show a person with the head of a bird and arms stretched out like wings. Of course, it's impossible for us to know exactly what the cave artist was thinking. But an ancient Greek myth contains a similar image. In the myth, a young boy, Icarus, escapes from the island of Crete by flying on artificial bird wings made of feathers and wax. When Icarus soars near the sun, the sun melts the wax and sets the wings on fire. Icarus then crashes into the sea. But the myth didn't send people's dream of flying into a meltdown. In the late 1800s, people built their first attempts at flying machines, with flapping devices that attached to the human body like bird wings. Too bad none of them really took off.

FACT TRACK

New Zealand owl

Barn owl

Owls swoop silently through the air to nab prey unawares. Gotcha! Their feathers have soft fringes that dampen the noise of air bumping up and down as it flows over their wings. Aircraft designers are even trying to copy owl wings for stealth airplanes.

93

BIRD WANNABES GET IN A FLAP

Orville Wright

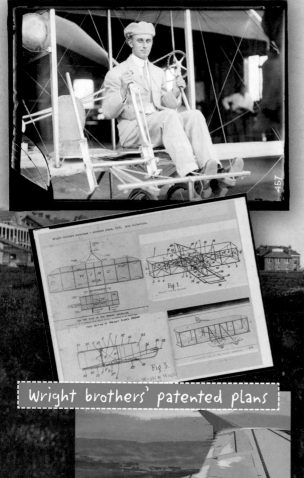

Wright brothers' patented plans

No matter how much people flapped imitation bird wings, they didn't get off the ground. But the inventors didn't give up. Eventually, they discovered that the secret of lift lies in the shape of a bird's wing. A bird's wing is curved on top and flat on the bottom. As the wing cuts through the air, air flows faster over the curved top of the wing than under the flat bottom. The slow-moving air at the bottom puts more pressure under the wing than the fast-moving air on top. And this difference in pressure lifts a bird up, up, and away! Once people realized this and made artificial wings the same shape as bird wings, flying machines began to take off too. In fact, the Wright brothers, who made the world's first flight in a powered airplane in 1903, studied the flight of turkey vultures to design the wings of their plane.

Birds also spread their feathers and change their wing shape to land. Modern airplanes have wings with flaps on the edges that pilots can raise and lower to land planes the same way. Talk about being in a flap!

The Jet Set Takes Off

H1N1 virus, a mircoscopic member of the jet set

As soon as people began soaring around the planet on board airplanes, the world seemed to get smaller. Suddenly, people were able to travel faster and farther than ever before. More and more people began traveling by air and shipping more cargo by air too. Jumbo jets that could carry the entire population of a small village—490 people, to be exact—across the Atlantic Ocean in a single flight soon followed. It became possible for people to travel and see the world just for leisure and pleasure. Jumbo jets kept getting bigger, and the age of the jet set was born. And do you know what that meant? Microbes—a.k.a. bugs, germs, and diseases (see page 82)—could hop, skip, and spread themselves around the world a lot more quickly. All the invisible bugs had to do was cling to the skin or guts of an unsuspecting traveler, and in just hours they could land halfway around the world in the midst of a whole new population of people ripe for infection. Who knew bugs were such jet-setters?

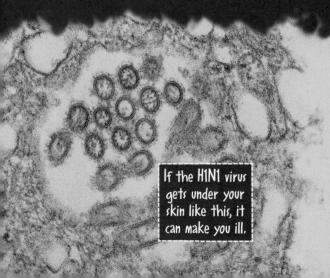

If the H1N1 virus gets under your skin like this, it can make you ill.

SPEAK OF THE BEAST

HAVE A BIRD

TO HAVE A SHOCK OR FIT. THE WORD BIRD IS SLANG FOR A "LOUD SOUND OF DISAPPROVAL." SO THIS EXPRESSION MAY COME FROM THE LOUD NOISES BIRDS MAKE AS THEY SQUAWK.

MAMMOTHS

Thousands of years ago, our Stone Age ancestors didn't hop on planes to see the world or even travel for pleasure. They got around on their own two feet following and hunting herds of big-game animals like mammoths that migrated with the change of seasons. Mammoths are extinct ancestors of modern-day elephants that had two long curved tusks. Check out how the big hairy beasts left their mark on the world.

Mammoth tusk

MUG SHOT

Names: Males are called "bulls," females "cows," and young ones "calves"

Domestication Date: Mammoths were never tamed.

Number in the World Today: None. Nearly 4,000 years ago, the last of the woolly mammoths died on Wrangel Island off the coast of Siberia, making the species extinct.

In the Wild: Herds of woolly mammoths thundered over the tundra of the northern hemisphere during the last Ice Age.

Claim to Fame: The flesh and bone of some woolly mammoths have been preserved in permafrost to reveal their nature to the modern world!

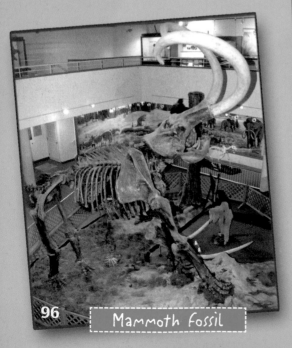

Mammoth Fossil

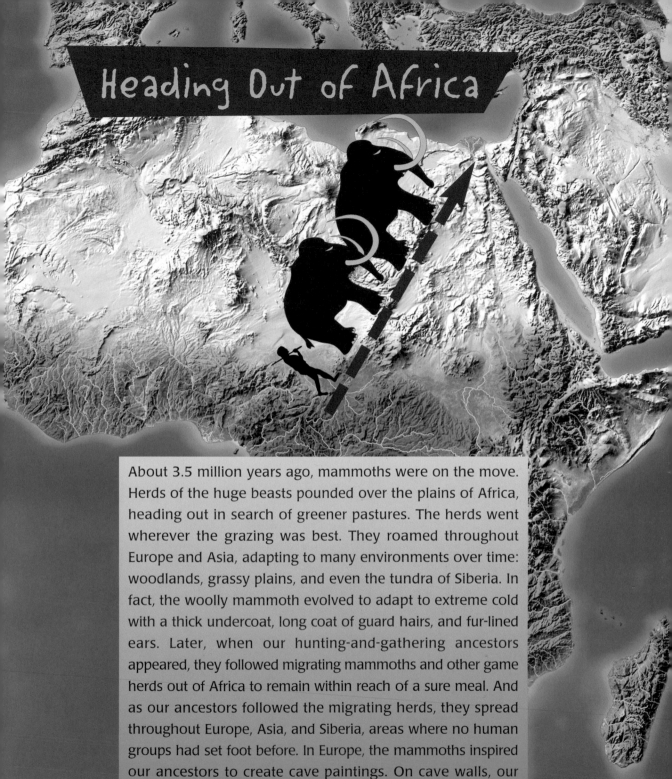

Heading Out of Africa

About 3.5 million years ago, mammoths were on the move. Herds of the huge beasts pounded over the plains of Africa, heading out in search of greener pastures. The herds went wherever the grazing was best. They roamed throughout Europe and Asia, adapting to many environments over time: woodlands, grassy plains, and even the tundra of Siberia. In fact, the woolly mammoth evolved to adapt to extreme cold with a thick undercoat, long coat of guard hairs, and fur-lined ears. Later, when our hunting-and-gathering ancestors appeared, they followed migrating mammoths and other game herds out of Africa to remain within reach of a sure meal. And as our ancestors followed the migrating herds, they spread throughout Europe, Asia, and Siberia, areas where no human groups had set foot before. In Europe, the mammoths inspired our ancestors to create cave paintings. On cave walls, our ancestors painted pictures of mammoth herds surging across the plains.

97

Mammoths Inspire Survival Gear

Mammoth fossil

Part of a mammoth tooth

The mammoths led our ancestors, early humans, all the way to Siberia. Along the way, our ancestors had to learn how to survive the harsh temperatures of cooler climates. Unlike woolly mammoths, they weren't covered in a thick coat of long hair that could keep them warm in temperatures as low as –29°Celsius (–20°Fahrenheit). But that didn't stop them from following and hunting the herds. They just looked to the mammoths for survival gear. For example, people of the Eastern Gravettian culture, who lived along the edge of glaciers in modern-day Russia, the Czech Republic, and Slovakia from 35,000 to 10,000 BCE, wore mammoth skins for warmth. They had no caves or rock shelters to live in. So they used needles made of bone to sew together mammoth skins and stretched the skins over polelike mammoth bones to build huts. They piled heavy mammoth bones around the outer edges of the huts, so strong winds wouldn't blow the huts away. Inside the huts, people kept fires burning for warmth, fueling the flames with mammoth tusks. And so woolly mammoths were a survival kit for the Ice Age, providing food, shelter, clothes, and warmth all in one big hairy package.

Mammoth footprints

Mammoths Discover North America

During the last Ice Age, the climate changed wildly. Temperatures rose and fell, affecting what plants could grow and where. In turn, this affected where mammoths could graze, where they migrated for food, and where human hunters followed in their hoof steps. About 25,000 years ago, scientists think a drop in temperature froze certain areas of the ocean. As the water level fell, a wide land bridge popped up between Siberia and Alaska. Waves of mammoth herds in search of new grazing grounds thudded over the bridge, with people hot on their heels. From there, they roamed south and east. And so mammoths led our ancient Stone Age ancestors into North America, a continent where no human had gone before.

IT'S A MAMMOTH PROBLEM.
IT'S HUGE. THIS EXPRESSION PROBABLY COMES FROM THE SHEER SIZE OF MAMMOTHS. AN ADULT BULL WAS ABOUT THREE TIMES AS TALL AS AN AVERAGE 10-YEAR-OLD KID.

SPEAK OF THE BEAST

DINOSAURS

Chances are you're more familiar with these gigantic creatures that ruled the Earth millions of years ago than with many creatures that exist today. But that wasn't always so. About 200 years ago, no one knew dinosaurs had ever roamed Earth. The name dinosaur didn't even exist. Check out how dinosaurs and their remains captured the imagination of the world.

Ceratosaurus nasicornis

Cearadactylus atrox

MUG SHOT

Names: "Dinos," short for "dinosaurs," which comes from the Greek word for "fearfully great lizard." Even though no dinosaurs were lizards and some were no bigger than a chicken, the name has stuck.

Domestication Date: Nonexistent. Dinosaurs lived more than 200 million years before people existed.

Number in the World Today: None. Dinosaurs became extinct about 65 million years ago. But some scientists argue that they are not actually extinct because some evolved into modern-day birds.

In the Wild: Dinosaurs were everywhere. They roamed all over Earth.

Claim to Fame: Dinosaurs were the biggest and longest-living land animals known on Earth.

Mamenchisaurus constructus

Who Owned This Huge Bone?

In the early 1800s, people stumbled upon fossils of huge teeth and gigantic bones. No one knew what creatures the fossils had come from. In fact, many people thought that the creatures must still exist somewhere in some unexplored corner of Earth. Back then it was unthinkable that any creature could become extinct. But as scientists used the fossil bones to reconstruct the animals, they debunked this myth. Some looked like massive reptiles larger than any known creature on Earth. In 1841, English scientist Richard Owen named them dinosaurs after the Greek word for "fearfully great lizard." In 1854, Owen helped build a dinosaur park of life-size models. And Dinomania was born, as hundreds of thousands of people flocked to see the model dinosaurs.

Dinosaur teeth

Dinosaur fossil

FACT TRACK

Don't think fossil fuels are the remains of dinosaurs. That's just a myth! Fossil fuels are the remains of plants and animals that lived millions of years before dinosaurs ever appeared on Earth.

THE BONE WARS

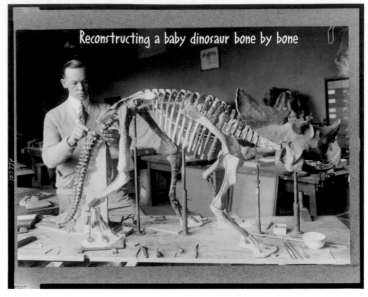
Reconstructing a baby dinosaur bone by bone

In the late 1800s, people remained fascinated with dinosaurs, and the Great Bone Rush was on! Bone hunters raced to see who could find the most fossils. They dug up great numbers of them and rushed to publish their discoveries. They put together bones and reconstructed dinosaurs, such as brontosaurus, triceratops, stegosaurus, and the long-necked reptile elasmosaurus. The science of paleontology sprung up, and over the years paleontologists uncovered the remains of dinosaurs all over Earth. Nevertheless, people didn't get bored of dino discoveries. "What did dinosaur skin look like?" people wondered. "What did they eat? How fast could they run? Where did they go? Were they warm-blooded or cold-blooded?" People had lots of questions and scientists fiercely debated the answers. (With no living specimens to study, many questions remain open to debate to this day.)

Wanna toot your own horn?
Don't call yourself a dinosaur, dude.

SPEAK OF THE BEAST

HE'S A DINOSAUR.
SOMEONE (OR SOMETHING) WHO'S COMPLETELY OUT OF DATE (OR OUT OF USE) BECAUSE HE HASN'T CHANGED WITH THE TIMES.

But some questions kept popping up that really got to people: "Why did the dinosaurs disappear? What wiped them off the face of Earth? If the dinosaurs died out—huge beasts that lived everywhere on Earth and virtually ruled the planet, like we do—could we disappear someday too?" Meanwhile, scientists put their heads together and tried to finger who—er, what—killed the dinos. Theories ranged from a killer bout of hay fever brought on by the appearance of flowering plants on the planet to the explosive impact of an asteroid striking Earth. Today, scientists think that global climate change was the culprit. Not able to adapt to changing temperatures, the dinosaurs died out along with many other animals in a mass extinction.

Scientists don't agree on what caused the change in climate, but the debate gets people thinking about the climate change taking place today. Even though climate change happens naturally, human activities like burning fossil fuels to heat our homes, power up computers, and run cars gives off greenhouse gases that add to it. In fact, many people think that if we don't want to go the way of the dinosaurs, if we want to stick around and have a world worth sticking around for, we better take care of the environment and reduce our role in global warming. So how will we change the world? As with any animal, only time will tell.

What Killed T. rex and Company?

Tyrannosaurus rex

ANIMALS DID WHAT?!

Charles Darwin

Blue-footed booby

Sally Lightfoot crab

Marine iguana

START A REVOLUTION

So maybe you've heard it's a dog-eat-dog world out there (see page 89) where "survival of the fittest" rules. Well, this idea didn't take the world by storm and become the norm until naturalist Charles Darwin sailed to the South Pacific in the 1800s and saw wonders few people had ever seen.

Back then, most people thought that animals could not change or adapt their bodies to changing environments over time. But during his travels, Darwin saw some animals that changed his mind. In South America, he uncovered fossils of extinct animals that looked so much like the armadillos and tree sloths living there that they could only be earlier forms of the same animals.

And in the Galapagos Islands, Darwin saw animals found nowhere else on Earth. The islands' 13 different species of finches particularly intrigued him. Only one species of this bird existed on the mainland of South America. So Darwin thought all the species must have originally come from there. Going island hopping, he discovered that the finches varied slightly from island to island. Then eventually, it hit him: the variations among the birds came from adaptations the species had made to their different island environments.

Darwin realized that every group of animals has physical variations, or differences, among them. As the animals struggle to survive, those with variations that give them an edge are the ones that survive to pass on the useful variations to their offspring. Over time, these characteristics become more common among the group and the species evolves.

And with that Darwin hit upon the theory of evolution. He wrote a book about it that sold out almost as soon as it was printed and got people talking everywhere. And so animals sparked Darwin to start a revolution that changed the way we think of all the world's species—including us.

If you visited the Galapagos Islands today, you might see some of these head-turning animals.

Further Reading

Aksomitis, Gerard, *Solving the Mysteries of the Past,* Crabtree Publishing Company, 2009.

Facklam, Margery, *Who Harnessed the Horse? The Story of Animal Domestication,* Little Brown, 1992.

Nosov, K., *War Elephants,* Osprey Publishing, 2008.

Rahn, Joan Elma, *Animals That Changed History,* Atheneum, 1986.

Ryden, Hope, *Out of the Wild: The Story of Domesticated Animals,* Lodestar Books, 1995.

Strauss, Rochelle, *Tree of Life: The Incredible Biodiversity of Life on Earth,* Kids Can Press, 2004.

Diamond, Jared, *Guns, Germs, and Steel: The Fates of Human Societies,* W. W. Norton & Company Ltd., 1999.

Gardiner, Juliet, *The Animals' War: Animals in Wartime from the First World War to the Present Day,* Portrait, 2006.

Grandin, Temple & Johnson, Catherine, *Animals Make Us Human: Creating the Best Life for Animals,* Houghton Mifflin Harcourt, 2009.

Houlihan, Patrick F., *The Animal World of the Pharaohs,* Thames and Hudson, The American University in Cairo Press, 1996.

Shubin, Neil, *Your Inner Fish: A Journey Into the 3.5-Billion-Year History of the Human Body,* Pantheon Books, 2008.

Selected Sources

Anthony, David W., *The Horse, the Wheel, and Language: How Bronze Age Riders from the Eurasian Steppes Shaped the Modern World,* Princeton University Press, 2007.

Caras, Roger A., *A Perfect Harmony: Intertwining Lives of Animals and Humans throughout History,* Simon & Schuster, 1996.

Clutton-Brock, Juliet, *A Natural History of Domesticated Mammals*, Cambridge University Press, 1999.

Steinfeld, Henning, Gerber, Pierre, Wassenaar, Tom, Castel, Vincent, Rosales, Mauricio, and de Haan, Cees, *Livestock's Long Shadow: Environmental Issues and Options*, Food and Agriculture Organization of the United Nations (FAO), 2006.

Wang, Xiaoming, *Dogs: Their Fossil Relatives and Evolutionary History,* Columbia University Press, 2008.

ANIMAL FOOTPRINTS IN TIME

Before 375,000,000 BCE A fish crawls out of the sea onto land where no creature has set fin or foot before. Over time, other animals follow, invading land around the world.

About 245,000,000 BCE Dinosaurs rule Earth.

About 66,000,000 BCE Dinosaurs become extinct.

About 4,000,000 BCE Human beings' earliest ancestors who walk on two feet emerge in Africa.

About 3,500,000 BCE Mammoths head out of Africa. Our ancient ancestors follow hot on their heels to stay within reach of hunt-'em-down meals.

About 25,000 BCE Mammoths discover North America as they roam across a land bridge over the ocean between Siberia and Alaska. Our ancient ancestors follow. And with that people set foot in North America for the first time.

About 13,000 BCE People domesticate, or tame, wolves. Eventually, wolves evolve into dogs—a.k.a. humankind's best friend.

About 8000 BCE Goats and sheep begin living in the company of people. People then have livestock on hand for meals and midnight snacks.

About 8000 to 3000 BCE People domesticate pigeons.

About 7500 BCE People domesticate cats.

About 7000 BCE People begin keeping guinea pigs as livestock.

About 4000 BCE People start milking cows.

About 4000 BCE People domesticate horses. Sooner or later, someone hops on the back of a horse, takes off for a ride, and riding horses becomes the fastest way for people to get around.

About 3500 BCE People domesticate silkworms, and silk fabric soon spins into the world.

About 2600 BCE People domesticate camels. Camels soon become "ships of the desert," helping people survive in dry, harsh areas where no human could live before.

About 2000 BCE The Silk Road becomes the longest road on Earth, as traders and caravans of camels carry silk out of China to the rest of the world at large.

776 BCE Pigeons deliver the results of the first Olympic Games.

77 CE Ivory from the tusks of elephants is all the rage in the Roman Empire, and Roman politician Pliny the Elder notices African elephants are vanishing.

945 CE Cats are made official guards of the king's grain in Wales.

From 1347 to 1351 CE Black rats spread the Black Death, or bubonic plague, across Europe. The plague slays 25 million people.

1497 CE Codfish are so plentiful off the shores of modern-day Newfoundland that European sailors can scoop them up by the bucketful.

1519 CE Horses arrive in North America from Spain and help people live in and tame the Wild West.

About 1600 CE Hats made of beaver fur become the "it" thing in Europe. In the quest to meet the demand for beaver fur, hunters and trappers explore, map, and settle North America.

1600s CE Codfish lure boatloads of English settlers to New England to make a living fishing.

1700s CE Flocks of sheep produce lots of wool, sparking the Industrial Revolution. People then produce massive amounts of goods, like sweaters, with machines.

1780 CE A French chemist uses guinea pigs to measure amounts of carbon dioxide and oxygen in breathing. Over the next 100 years, the small rodents become the lab animal of choice.

Early 1800s CE People stumble on fossils of huge teeth and giant bones that don't come from any living creature on Earth. It takes years to put the pieces together to reconstruct models of dinosaurs.

1908 CE The Wright brothers study wings of birds for the secret of flight and use what they learn to design the world's first airplane that gets off the ground.

1914 CE Pigeons are the world's fastest and most reliable way to send a message. As World War I breaks out, both the Allies and the Germans use the birds to deliver important news and messages.

About 1945 to 1991 CE During the Cold War, the United States and the former Soviet Union use dolphins to guard their navy bases.

1992 CE Codfish are so scarce off the shores of Newfoundland that Canada bans cod fishing.

Today Elephants, long gone from many parts of the world, and their endangered pals, giant pandas, are poster beasts for the world's endangered species.

Photo Credits

Front cover, 58 left top, Vladimir Mucibabic; speech bubbles, Triggerjoy and Ken Toh; 1, Ilia Shcherbakov; 2, Michael Pettigrew; 3 second left, 25 left, Distinctiveimages; 3 third left, Sebastian Kaulitzki; 3 fourth left, Pniesen; 3 top right, Ruth Black; 3 second right, Linda Bucklin; 3 third right, Saeid Shahin Kiya; 6, Judwick; 7 left, Photoeupho; 7 top right, Terence Mendoza; 7 middle right, Ukrphoto; 7 bottom right, Stuart Miles; 8 top, back cover right, Nikolay Petkov; 8 middle, Alexander Mychko; 8 bottom, Michael Elliott; 8 bottom background, Gkuna; 9 top, Daniela Schraml; 9 bottom, Steve Cukrov; 9 bottom background, Dgrilla; 10 middle, Basphoto; 11 top, Imaani1000; 11 bottom left, Eduard Kachan; 11 bottom right, Posztós János; 12 top left, Lorna; 12 middle left, Derrick Neill; 12 bottom left, Joe Gough; 12 right, Drbouz; 14 left, Matthew Collingwood; 14 top right, Peterdenov; 14 middle right, Edyta Pawlowska; 14 bottom right, Robert Balazik; 15 top left, Lucian Coman; 15 middle left, Christian Noval; 15 bottom left, Stephen Coburn; 15 top right, Werner Münzker; 15 middle right, Falcon stock; 15 bottom right, Yuriy Chaban; 16 top left and right, Johan Siggesson; 16 middle left, Moanra; 16 bottom left, Jan Gerrit Siesling; 16 middle right, Withgod; 16 bottom right, Steve Degenhardt; 17 left, Shailesh Nanal; 17 top right, Dennis Cox; 17 bottom right, Etiamos; 18 bottom, Geraldine Doran; 19 top left, Hywit Dimyadi; 19 bottom left, Laurent Renault; 19 top right, Josef Muellek; 19 bottom right, Feng Yu; 20 top left, Georgios Kollidas; 20 top right, Giuseppe Ramos; 20 bottom left, Ahmet Ihsan Ariturk; 20 bottom middle, Piotr Antonów; 20 bottom right, Abdullah Sm; 21 top left, Eric Isselée; 21 bottom left, Eriklam; 21 top right, Glenda Powers; 21 bottom right, Tad Denson; 22 top left, John Betancur; 22 middle left, Fultonsphoto; 22 bottom left, Kitchner Bain; 22 right, Spauln; 23 top first, Mila Dimova; 23 top second, Cynoclub; 23 bottom left, Heinz Effner; 23 bottom right, Andy Piat; 24 top left, Anna Utekhina; 24 middle left, Eric Isselée; 24 bottom left, Kateleigh; 24 right, Eric Isselée; 25 right, Galina Barskaya; 25 background, Shilo Long; 26 left top, Zts; 26 left bottom, Vladimir Wrangel; 26 center, Kristian Sekulic; 26 right top, 26 right second, 26 right third, Eric Isselée; 26 right bottom, Misad; 27 left bottom, Carlos Arranz; 27 left bottom background, Stuart Welburn; 27 right bottom, Ami Beyer; 28 left top, Ruslandashinsky; 28 left bottom, Fromout; 28 right top, Georgios Kollidas; 28 right bottom, Chris Lorenz; 29 top, Alvaro Pantoja; 29 left, Linncurrie; 29 right, Linda Bucklin; 29 background, Jennifer Thompson; 30 left top, Anett Bakos; 30 right top, Igor Dutina; 31 left top, Michael Zysman; 31 left bottom, Steven Wynn and David Campbell; 31 right, Igor Dutina and Karammiri; 32 top, Sierpniowka; 32 middle, Oliver Suckling; 32 bottom, Diman Oshchepkov; 33 top, Branko Kosteski; 33 right, Jozsef Szasz-Fabian and Flynt; 34 top, Grigory Smirnov; 34 background, Chad Mcdermott; 35 top, Suprijono Suharjoto; 35 middle, Dmitrijs Dmitrijevs; 35 background, Jen Shuang Wong; 36 middle, Seesea; 36 background, Mihail Syarov; 37 bottom, Stuart Welburn; 38 bottom, Vladislav Ociacia; 39 middle, Jordano; 39 background, Naci Yavuz; 40 top left, Hongqi Zhang; 40 bottom left, Li Su; 40 top right, Greg Amptman; 40 bottom right, Pmstock; 41 middle, Steven Wright; 41 left bottom, Oleg Kozlov; 42 background, 4c4j4s; 42 bottom, Qtrix; 43 bottom left, Jörg Beuge; 43 right top and middle, Sebastian Czapnik; 43 right bottom, Rene Drouyer; 44 middle, Popescu Iacob Emanuel; 45 left bottom, Rosamund Parkinson; 45 right top, 46 bottom, Pancaketom; 46 background, Nikolay Okhitin; 49 third, Navarone; 49 fourth, Jasonyerface; 50 top, Nancy Tripp; 50 middle first, Michael Elliott; 50 middle second, Pindiyath100; 50 middle third, Kitchner Bain; 50 middle fourth, Nico Smit; 50 bottom, lillisphotography; 51 top, Maksym Gorpenyuk; 51 middle, Scott Griessel; 51 bottom, Bornholm; 52 top, Batuque and Radist777; 53 background, Seesea; 54 left top, Andy-kim Möller; 54 right top, Vladyslav Morozov; 54 middle, Tomas Hajek; 55 middle, Robertplotz; 55 bottom, Vera Volkova; 55 background, Lenice Harms; 56 top third, Stocksnapper; 57 top, Robertplotz; 58 left middle and left bottom, Andymak; 58 right top, Jinfeng Zhang; 58 right bottom, Paul Prescott; 59 left, Martin Mcmillan; 59 middle, Dario Bajurin; 59 right, Anna Claesson; 59 background, Mypix; 60 top, Andriy Bezuglov; 60 top background, Ronald Van Der Beek; 61 left bottom, Carolyne Pehora; 61 right bottom, Jeremyrichards; 62 left top and 62 right bottom, Duncan Noakes; 62 right top, Musat Christian; 62 middle, Duncan Noakes; 62 left and middle bottom, Goce Risteski; 63 bottom, Martin Vrlik; 63 top background, Gualtiero Boffi; 63 bottom background, Iwona joanna Rajszczak; 64 bottom, Dennis Cox; 64 bottom background, Janaka Dharmasena; 65 top, Chris Fourie; 65 bottom left, Teamcrucillo; 65 bottom right, Francois Lariviere; 66 top, Musat Christian; 66 bottom, Lynne Williamson; 67 middle, Philip Lange; 69 top, Petr Nikolaevich; 69 first right, Tom Dowd; 69 second right, Michael Price; 69 bottom, Thor Jorgen Udvang; 70 top, Meccano; 71 bottom, Andreus; 72 top, Ragnarock; 72 middle left, Misha Shiyanov; 72 middle right, Miflippo; 73 top, Michael Zysman; 74 bottom right, Rick Thornton; 74 background, Nikolay Okhitin; 75 top, Annie Beland; 75 middle, Cathy Keifer; 75 bottom, Aniram; 76 top, Knorre; 76 middle left, Ew Chee Guan; 76 middle right, Marco Vatteroni; 77 top, Bernhard Schiestel; 77 middle, Vinicius Tupinamba; 77 bottom, Kaikai; 78 fourth right, Simon Krzic; 79 top right, Petra Roeder; 79 bottom, Wouter Tolenaars; 80 bottom left, Alexandr Kalinkin; 80 bottom right, Ilia Shcherbakov; 81 top, Linqong; 81 bottom background, Sebastian Kaulitzki; 82 top left, Franz Pfluegl; 82 top right, Christos Georghiou; 82 middle, Imagez; 82 bottom, Matt Jacques; 84 top, Gnanavel Subramani; 84 middle, Brian Santa Maria; 84 bottom, Jamie Wilson; 85 top left, Julien Trombini; 85 top right, Kurt; 85 top background, Mauro Rodrigues; 85 bottom second, Marek Chalupník; 85 bottom third, Sgame; 86 top, Dallasphotography; 86 middle, Janet Lo; 86 bottom, Mailthepic; 86 background, Sarah Theophilus; 87 top, Diego Barucco; 87 middle, Lihui; 88 top, Woodooart; 88 bottom, Nadezhda Bolotina; 88 background, Paul Maguire; 89 top, Dmitry Kolesnikov; 89 bottom, Spland06; 89 background, Ariel Bravy; 90 top, Andreas Meyer; 90 middle, Lars Christensen; 90 bottom, Kevin Renes; 91 top, Ingrid Prats; 91 middle, Henrique Araujo; 91 bottom, Markbeckwith; 92 top, Roberto Okamura; 92 middle left, Yury Shirokov; 92 middle right, Jason Stitt; 92 bottom, Igor Shypitsyn; 92 background, Mike Tan; 93 top first, Madartists; 93 bottom left, Eric Isselée; 93 bottom right, Christopher Moncrieff; 93 bottom background, Federico Donatini; 94 fourth, Marcelmooij; 95 top left, Norebbo; 95 top right, 2ndpic; 95 bottom right, Wetnose1; 97, Michael Schmeling and Grzegorz Japol and Kevin Renes; 99 left, Grzegorz Japol; 99 bottom, Monika Wisniewska; 100, Michal Adamczyk; 101 bottom, Jun Mu; 102 bottom left, Andreas Meyer; 102 bottom right, Dawn Hudson; 103 right, Linda Bucklin; 103 background, Ben Goode; 104 second, Thorsten Folk; 104 third, Morten Elm; 104 fourth, Michael Zysman; 104 background, Justin Black; 106 top, Linda Bucklin; 106 middle, Jozef Sedmak; 106 background, Bram Janssens; 106 bottom, 107 bottom, 108 bottom, 109 bottom, Gabor Weisz; 107 top, Donkeyru; 107 middle, Iconspro; 107 background, Janaka Dharmasena; 108 first, Joe Mercier; 108 second, Stuart Welburn; 109 first, Orientaly; 109 third, Spooky2006; 109 background, Peterdenov; ©Dreamstime.com. 3 fourth right, 68 bottom right, U.S. Navy: Pierre G. Georges; 68 top, back cover left, U.S. Marine Corps: Cpl. Paula M. Fitzgerald; 67 top, 68 bottom left, U.S. Navy: Brien Aho; 67 bottom, U.S. Navy: S. L. Standifird; 70 bottom, American Expeditionary Forces. 9 middle; 10 top; 10 bottom, left; 11 middle left and right; 13 top, bottom; 30 right bottom; 34 bottom; 37 top; 41 right bottom; 45 right bottom; 46 top; 47 top; 47 bottom; 48 top; 48 bottom; 49 bottom; 52 bottom; 53 left bottom; 53 right bottom; 53 right top; 54 bottom; 56 top first; 56 top second; 56 bottom; 57 bottom; 63 middle; 64 top; 71 top; 73 bottom left; 78 second; 78 third; 78 fourth left; 93 top second; 104 first; 109 second; back cover bottom: ©2010 Jupiterimages Corporation. 18 top, Josef Muellek; 33 bottom, Smokeyjo; 35 bottom, eylon steiner; 36 top, BMPix; 36 bottom, Dori OConnell; 37 background, 48 background, Günay Mutlu; 38 top, Vickie Sichau; 38 background, Jamie Carroll; 39 top, Richard Cano; 44 top, kawisign; 44 bottom, yenwen; 45 left top, PeaceLilyPhotography; 49 top, dennysb; 49 second, Miha Urbanija; 60 bottom, Brandon Laufenberg; 60 bottom background, Xiaoping Liang; 61 middle, HultonArchive; 65 background, Cliff Parnell; 66 middle, Nancy Nehring; 72 bottom, peregrine; 73 bottom right, Cathy Keifer; 76 bottom, Paul Pegler; 79 top left, Milos Peric; 80 top, graham klotz; 81 bottom, Ryan Lane; 83 left, JulienGrondin; 83 right, shuchun ke; 96 top, Olga Belyaeva; 96 middle, reanas; 98 top, A-Digit; 98 middle, Jake Holmes; 98 bottom, KIM FREITAS; 99 background, Dmitry Goygel-Sokol; 101 middle, Wesley Pohl; 103 left, jamesbenet: ©iStockphoto Inc. 27 top, ©The Art Archive/Musée du Louvre, Paris/Gianni Dagli Orti. 28 left middle, imageZebra-Fotolia.com. 30 left bottom, 01113750©Gabriel Rojo/naturepl.com. 41 bottom, NOAA, courtesy National Archives. 3 top left; 55 top; 57 middle; 108 third: Beinecke Rare Book and Manuscript Library. 61 top, Australian War Memorial Negative Number P03631.007. 63 top, 94 first, http://commons.wikimedia.org. 65 middle; 78 first; 94 second; 94 third; 101 top; 102 top: Library of Congress. 74 top, John Montenieri; 74 bottom left, 85 bottom first; 81 top background, Bobby Strong; 84 background, F. A. Murphy; 95 bottom left, C. Goldsmith, D. Rollin: CDC. 87 bottom, Zina Deretsky, National Science Foundation. 96 bottom, 2001 S.W. Clyde. 99 right, Mark A. Wilson, The College of Wooster.

110

Index